Instructor's Manual to accompany

Assoziationen
Deutsch für die Mittelstufe

Ronald W. Walker
Colorado State University

Erwin Tschirner
University of Iowa

Brigitte Nikolai
University of Iowa

Gerhard F. Strasser
The Pennsylvania State University

McGraw-Hill, Inc.
New York   St. Louis   San Francisco   Auckland   Bogotá   Caracas   Hamburg
Lisbon   London   Madrid   Mexico   Milan   Montreal   New Delhi   Paris
San Juan   São Paulo   Singapore   Sydney   Tokyo   Toronto

This is an  book.

Instructor's Manual to accompany
Assoziationen

Copyright © 1991 by McGraw-Hill, Inc. All rights reserved. Printed in the United States of America. The contents, or parts thereof, may be reproduced without permission, solely for use with *Assoziationen* by Ronald Walker et al., provided such reproductions carry the same copyright herein, but may not be reproduced, or distributed, for any other pupose, without the prior written permission of the publisher.

      3 4 5 6 7 8 9 0   HAN HAN   9 5 4 3 2

ISBN: 0-07-557372-5

This instructor's manual was formatted on a Macintosh computer by Fog Press.
The editors were Leslie Berriman and Gregory Trauth.
The production manager was Fred Martich.
Production and editorial assistance were provided by Stacey Sawyer.
Hamilton Reproductions, Inc., was the printer and binder.

Contents

I. Introduction *1*
   Ancillary Materials *1*
   Organizational Principles *2*
   Teaching for Proficiency *4*
   Pedagogical Principles *7*
   Readings and Reading Strategies *7*
   Writing and Writing Strategies *8*
   Implementing Small Group Activities *8*
   Working with Dialogues *8*
   Error Correction *9*
   Presentation and Role of Vocabulary *10*
   Presentation and Role of Grammar *10*
II. Chapter Notes *15*
   A Step-by-Step Guide to Working with Readings, Visuals, and Activities *15*
   Einführungskapitel *15*
   Thema I *21*
   Kapitel 1 *21*
   Kapitel 2 *27*
   Kapitel 3 *32*
   Thema II *37*
   Kapitel 4 *37*
   Kapitel 5 *40*
   Kapitel 6 *43*
   Thema III *48*
   Kapitel 7 *48*
   Kapitel 8 *53*
   Kapitel 9 *58*
   Thema IV *62*
   Kapitel 10 *62*
   Kapitel 11 *65*
   Kapitel 12 *68*

        Thema V   *71*
        Kapitel 13   *72*
        Kapitel 14   *75*
        Kapitel 15   *77*
III. Appendix   *81*
        ACTFL Proficiency Guidelines   *81*

I

INTRODUCTION

Assoziationen is an intermediate college-level textbook whose format and content are geared toward students who, after two or more years of high school study or one year of college study, have acquired a knowledge of basic German vocabulary and grammar. With its emphasis on proficiency in the four skills of reading, writing, listening, and speaking, as well as on sociocultural competence, *Assoziationen* provides instructors with a second-year German program ideally suited to the proficiency-oriented classroom.

The college-level intermediate German course typically attracts students from a variety of learning backgrounds and with varying levels of proficiency. These students all need to review and refine their understanding of structures, broaden their active and passive vocabularies, and probe more deeply the culture and literature of the German-speaking peoples. In addition, students need to feel successful at this stage of language development. As instructors, we must give them the opportunity to reinforce and use, in meaningful contexts and with minimal stress, what they have learned. *Assoziationen* and its ancillaries were specifically designed, with recognition of these needs, to facilitate language teaching and language learning at the intermediate level.

Ancillary Materials

Several ancillaries accompany *Assoziationen*:

- *Arbeitsbuch*, a combined workbook and laboratory manual
- *Audiocassette Program* with dialogues for listening comprehension
- *McGraw-Hill Electronic Language Tutor (MHELT)*, a computer program consisting of the single response exercises from the *Arbeitsbuch*
- *Visual Materials and Activities*, (VMA), containing transparency masters of art from the textbook and additional realia and activities
- *McGraw-Hill Video Library of Authentic German Materials, Vol. I: A German TV Journal,* including an *Instructor's Guide* and featuring authentic segments from German television (**ZDF**)
- *Color Slides*
- this *Instructor's Manual*

The *Arbeitsbuch*, with its listening comprehension, vocabulary, grammar, and writing exercises, is an integral part of the *Assoziationen* program. It corresponds closely to the textbook with respect to themes, vocabulary, and structures but offers additional writing activities, as well as reading and writing strategies. Unlike the textbook, which is designed mainly for classroom instruction, the *Arbeitsbuch* is meant for practice and study outside class. An answer key is provided at the end of the *Arbeitsbuch* for the listening comprehension and standard-response vocabulary and grammar exercises.

The *Audiocassette Program* contains authentic-sounding dialogues for listening comprehension that are tied thematically to the textbook. Because the dialogues emphasize sociocultural content, instructors are encouraged to listen to the tapes and use the dialogues as a point of departure for classroom discussions. Indeed, many of the dialogues present unique, and sometimes controversial, perspectives on the culture and societies of the German-speaking peoples. The *Audiocassette Program* is provided free to adopting institutions; additionally, students can purchase the audiocassettes for personal use. A tapescript is available for instructors.

The *McGraw-Hill Electronic Language Tutor (MHELT)* is a computer-assisted learning program designed for institutions having a computer laboratory. Self-correcting and providing immediate feedback, this program also relieves the teacher of correcting the standard-response vocabulary and grammar exercises. An inviting way to learn German, the computer program appeals especially to students who are more visually than verbally oriented.

The *Visual Materials and Activities* (VMA) was compiled especially for instructors who use overhead projectors or handouts in their class or who desire fresh realia and activities. The VMA materials, printed as high-quality masters for transparencies or photocopies, are especially suited for group or class work. Many of the line drawings from the textbook have been included to give instructors more flexibility in certain activities.

The *McGraw-Hill Video Library of Authentic German Materials, Vol. I: A German TV Journal* and the *Color Slides* can be easily integrated into your lesson plans. The *Instructor's Guide* that accompanies the video gives practical hints for incorporating the video in class activities. Authentic and engaging, the video segments and the slides offer students an interesting and delightful diversion from regular class activities.

This *Instructor's Manual* presents an overview of the underlying organizational principles of the textbook, describes the goals of the proficiency movement and its implications for an intermediate proficiency-oriented course, summarizes the pedagogical principles of the textbook, and provides extra guidance and alternatives for exploiting the activities, artwork, photographs, and realia in the textbook. In addition, this manual provides the instructor with a wealth of cultural information. These practical ideas will help you to get the most out of *Assoziationen*. Both novice and seasoned instructors who may not have had much experience with proficiency-oriented instruction should find the suggestions useful for planning their daily lessons.

Organizational Principles

The textbook consists of an introductory chapter and five units (**Themen I–V**), each of which comprises three chapters that treat different facets of a broader unit theme. Opening photographs set the themes for the five units and the fifteen regular chapters and, together with their summarizing captions, provide a basis for initial discussion and introductory activities. Like the supporting realia and artwork throughout the textbook, the photographs are meant to be integrated into instruction. This *Instructor's Manual* offers suggestions for using the photographs to introduce chapter themes and to promote student interest in the subject matter.

Following the opening photograph is an overview of chapter contents that lists the readings (**Texte**), language functions (**Sprechakte**), vocabulary (**Wortschatz**), and grammar points (**Strukturen**). Functional descriptions, given in English, of the points covered in the last three sections illuminate the relationship between the materials and the proficiency goals of the chapter. The overview provides students with both an orientation to and a checklist of language-learning goals.

Each chapter is organized as follows:

Einstimmung: Advance organizer
Lesetext: Introduction to the reading
Vor dem Lesen: Reading strategies and prereading activities
Text: Reading
Nach dem Lesen: Postreading activities
Aktivitäten: Core activities
Sprechakte: Language functions
Variationen: Language function activities
Und jetzt zu Ihnen!: Role-playing
Wortschatz: Vocabulary
Strukturen: Grammar

As the advance organizer, the **Einstimmung** provides a visual preview of the chapter theme. The visuals, usually realia or line drawings, are accompanied by questions for pair, group, or class discussion that orient the students within the theme and stimulate their creative and associative capabilities. In addition, the introductory discussion of the chapter theme offers students the opportunity to recall previously learned vocabulary and structures, which smooths the transition to the readings and their related activities. The instructor should check students' proficiency as they start to work with the new topic and its related functions. Suggestions for this can be found in this instructor's manual.

The prereading section, **Vor dem Lesen,** gives background information on the subject and the author of the reading and presents strategies that aid students in reading in an active and engaged manner. Prereading activities teach students how to use the linguistic and cultural context, the skills of skimming and scanning, and selective decoding to enhance their understanding of the text. Some prereading activities in *Assoziationen* include predicting the content of a reading from its title or from nonverbal clues in the accompanying illustrations, recognizing cognates, understanding stage directions in a play, or brainstorming to reactivate the students' background knowledge about the particular subject.

Each chapter contains two or more reading selections—the number depending on length and difficulty. Since the reading strategies are designed to lead to independent reading of unglossed texts, the readings have been glossed as little as possible. Heinz Oehler's *Grund- und Aufbauwortschatz Deutsch als Fremdsprache* was used as the basis for determining which words should be glossed.

In the postreading activities, appearing under the heading **Nach dem Lesen,** students work with the text they have just read. Among other activities, students organize and categorize information, give personal reactions to statements or passages, expand vocabulary, summarize and analyze the text, and discuss the content of the reading. The postreading activities develop students' proficiency in the four skills and broaden their understanding and appreciation of sociocultural matters.

The **Aktivitäten** are sequenced, moving from controlled and guided to more open-ended. Tying in to the general chapter theme, they serve as a bridge from the readings to the functional–situational activities, or **Sprechakte**.

The language functions presented in the **Sprechakte** provide students with additional linguistic tools to communicate appropriately and successfully in various situations they might encounter in a German-speaking country. Pragmatically oriented dialogues illustrate situations in which particular language functions, such as expressing disappointment or making requests, typically occur. In performing the accompanying activities, or **Variationen,** students draw possible and relevant vocabulary and phrases from a stock of useful expressions.

The **Sprechakte** culminate in a section entitled **Und jetzt zu Ihnen!,** which sets up plausible role-playing situations. Among other things, the role plays may require students to maneuver through difficult situations, solve conflicts, change a particular state of affairs, elicit a particular response from someone, or cause someone to carry out a particular action. The role plays are designed as pair activities.

In keeping with the conceptual focus of the textbook, the themes and language functions establish thematic categories for the chapter vocabulary, or **Wortschatz.** Unlike other textbooks, in which vocabulary items are listed according to parts of speech, *Assoziationen* organizes vocabulary in four semantic categories per chapter that correspond to the chapter themes, readings, and activities. Within each "semantic field," vocabulary items have been grouped according to level. The subsection entitled **Das wissen Sie schon** reviews basic, or "first-year," vocabulary without English translations, whereas more advanced expressions, accompanied by English translations, fall under the subsection called **Das ist neu.** Expressions from the **Sprechakte** also appear in the **Wortschatz,** thus consolidating all "vocabulary to be learned" in one place. The vocabulary lists are introduced by questions that stimulate the reactivation of the vocabulary. In addition, the *Arbeitsbuch* contains extra vocabulary exercises for each list.

Approximately eighty words per chapter, chosen from Heinz Oehler's *Grund- und Aufbauwortschatz Deutsch als Fremdsprache* constitute the active core vocabulary of each chapter. Vocabulary is practiced extensively, appearing not only in the readings and activities but also in the taped dialogues and vocabulary and grammar exercises in the *Arbeitsbuch*. By the end of the course, instructors may assume that students have an active vocabulary of at least 2000 words, with a much larger passive vocabulary.

Although not considered the focal point of instruction, grammar provides the underpinning for the communicative activities in the textbook. Structures and functions from the chapter readings and activities establish the grammatical categories treated in the grammar explanations. Thus, the grammar explanations, or **Strukturen,** are conceived both syntactically and semantically. For example, the subjunctive is presented in stages according to its various uses; and concessives, whether conjunctions, prepositions, or adverbs, are handled together. In this way, students acquire analogous structures that enhance their repertoires and encourage sensitivity to stylistic variation.

The **Strukturen** have been written in English so that students can work through the grammar on their own. This approach toward grammar instruction is carried one step further, in that all grammar exercises appear in the *Arbeitsbuch*, making this supplement an integral part of the *Assoziationen* program. The answer key in the *Arbeitsbuch* allows students to check their own work on completion, thereby enabling them to practice grammar on their own. More detailed information on the grammatical approach can be found below in the section on the Presentation and Role of Grammar.

Teaching for Proficiency

Teaching for proficiency has been a goal of the United States government and military language schools for more than three decades, and many foreign language instructors in colleges and universities have embraced it enthusiastically as a goal for their own classes. During the 1980s, as the proficiency movement was widely discussed and its findings implemented in the classroom, foreign language teaching took on new dimensions. Although much of the discussion centered on oral proficiency, proficiency is not, of course, limited to oral production; rather, it also applies to reading, writing, and listening, and includes cultural competence as well.

When a major goal of studying a foreign language is learning to communicate in that language, the act of teaching takes on a new dimension. When communicating in the language, as well as learning about it, is important, instructors must structure classroom activities to develop students' proficiency. The focus on teaching students to communicate in the foreign language has shifted the emphasis in teaching materials and methods to those that further proficiency goals. This part of the *Instructor's Manual* describes the kinds of input that lead most effectively to proficiency.

In a traditional classroom, students learn the structures and the vocabulary of each lesson and are expected to produce them in controlled exercises done in class, under the watchful eye of the instructor, and on tests in controlled situations (for example, discrete item exercises). This kind of testing, which focuses on specific structures and vocabulary, is called "achievement testing." When the class moves on to the next chapter, however, many instructors note that little of what has been taught in previous chapters is actually used by students in free conversation or in written assignments. What is lacking is the transition from language learning to language production in realistic contexts.

"Achievement" refers to a limited body of material: a specific chapter of the textbook, several chapters, all the verbs in the preceding five chapters, and so on. Since what is examined on an achievement test can be clearly delineated, students who have carefully studied the proposed materials have a chance of knowing everything on the test and getting a perfect score. Achievement tests measure only what has been previously presented in class or in a book. They can be given in written or oral form.

Proficiency, however, focuses not on the covered material but on specific skills. A score on a proficiency test indicates how well the candidate has done compared to all others who have the tested skill. In a test of oral proficiency, the body of material is infinite, and a wide variety of questions is asked; few restrictions are placed on the possible content of the test. In fact, most of the questions would probably deal with material other than the specific material that the candidate has studied. Proficiency is, therefore, a measure of how well one uses the language at a given moment, not how well one has learned the material of a specific chapter or course.

Proficiency often lags far behind achievement. When students are in a small group in class or with German-speaking friends outside the classroom, they are usually unable to sustain narration and description in the past, even though they can accurately produce the past tense on an achievement test. Thus, their proficiency is not at the same level as their academic achievement as reflected in test scores. All the input of the classroom has resulted in a very small amount of output, or proficiency.

We do not intend to suggest that work toward students' achievement be abandoned. Attention to both proficiency and achievement is important. The heart of proficiency-based teaching lies in presenting material to students for a functional purpose, in a sequence that reflects a natural learning order, and in a form that will make it more readily useful in real-life language situations.

The Proficiency Guidelines developed by the American Council on the Teaching of Foreign Languages (ACTFL) and the Educational Testing Service (ETS) describe all levels of language proficiency from "Novice" to "Superior." Proficiency is measured in ranges of increasing ability in speaking, listening, reading, and writing. The rating in each area takes into account ability in grammar and pronunciation as well as fluency and sociolinguistic knowledge. Performance at each level is summarized below. See the appendix for the complete guidelines.

The ACTFL Proficiency Guidelines identify four major levels of linguistic development. These levels and their subdivisions are as follows:

Superior

Advanced High
Advanced

Intermediate High
Intermediate Mid
Intermediate Low

Novice High
Novice Mid
Novice Low

The proficiency goals of an intermediate language course must be reasonable and attainable, so that students have a chance to succeed. Some students in a proficiency-oriented second-year college course can be expected to reach the ACTFL/ETS Advanced level if both textbook and instructor provide opportunities for them to do so.

The term "Intermediate" is used here in reference to the ACTFL/ETS rating scale. The terms "Novice," "Intermediate," and "Advanced" do not correspond to the curricular terms of beginning, intermediate, and advanced German. By the end of first-year German, most students in a proficiency-oriented classroom will be in the higher end of the ACTFL/ETS Intermediate range in reading and listening, and there or just below (Intermediate Low) in speaking and writing. During the intermediate-level course, all skills should progress further within the ACTFL/ETS Intermediate range. *Assoziationen* has been designed to help students develop their proficiency from that base level. Here is a list of specific proficiency goals for second-year students:

- Develop a large body of active vocabulary and begin to acquire strategies for circumlocution
- Ask and answer questions
- Build accuracy with common structures
- Begin to lengthen utterances and group them into paragraphs or narratives
- Survive a situation with a complication—that is, cope with an unpredictable event
- Narrate and understand narration in present, past, and future time (speaking, reading, writing, listening)
- Describe and understand description in present, past, and future time
- Begin to support opinions, hypothesize, and talk about abstract topics
- Participate in conversations about concrete topics and current events

By focusing on the Intermediate High range, we do not mean to suggest that it is the endpoint of desired proficiency. Colleagues critical of proficiency as an organizing principle for the foreign language curriculum sometimes perceive, erroneously, that all that is contemplated is a survival, tourist-level mastery of German. In fact, we hope students will reach the Intermediate or Advanced level of proficiency and attain the speaking, listening, reading, and writing skills required for upper-division courses.

Following the ACTFL guidelines, this book emphasizes a balanced approach to the teaching of function, context, and accuracy. Function describes what the speaker/writer can do linguistically in the target language; context describes the topics that can be discussed and the vocabulary that can be used; accuracy describes the degree of correctness of grammar and pronunciation. No one aspect is stressed to the detriment of another.

Here are the eleven basic functions, the mastery of which is necessary to progress up the ACTFL oral proficiency scale:

1. asking and answering questions
2. describing in present time
3. narrating in present time
4. surviving a simple (predictable) situation
5. describing in past time
6. narrating in past time
7. surviving a complicated (unpredictable) situation
8. describing in future time
9. narrating in future time
10. supporting opinion
11. hypothesizing

Each unit of this text targets several of these functions, progressing from the simplest to the more complex. The functions provide a focal point for the communication activities, the grammatical presentations, the exercises, and the reading and writing practice, even if not explicitly stated. The units and chapters of *Assoziationen* are structured so that the key functions are presented and developed in a cyclical fashion. At no time is any function dropped from the student's repertoire. Once functions have been presented, they recur regularly in varying combinations. Every activity in the unit—reading, listening comprehension exercises, directed writing exercises, and role playing, among others—involve these functions.

This strategy aims to enhance students' confidence in their ability to master the most basic functions at the same time they are beginning to acquire the more difficult ones. No one would want to claim that all students studying German in this way would be able to reach the Advanced level in one year. However, it is likely that with such a systematic process of reentry and reinforcement of the functions required for an ACTFL rating of Intermediate or Advanced, most college students should be able to reach the Intermediate High level by the end of the second year. Some exceptional students may even reach the Advanced level.

Some basic teaching strategies can help students achieve proficiency goals:

- Repeat new vocabulary frequently within each chapter
- Recycle vocabulary from chapter to chapter
- Personalize materials
- Contextualize materials
- Design activities with informational gaps, so that students must communicate real information
- Do role playing
- Do only controlled or limited error correction
- Nurture class atmosphere
- Do frequent pair and small-group work with communicative activities
- Use the target-language exclusively
- Use activities that integrate skills

Clearly, no single second-year German textbook is best for teachers who consider proficiency the organizing principle in their classrooms. Many texts can be adapted to meet proficiency goals. However, what is special about *Assoziationen* is that its authors are especially well versed in the assumptions and goals of the proficiency movement and have been trained as ACTFL oral-proficiency testers. Thus, although *Assoziationen* was conceived to be a versatile intermediate course independent of specific schools of language teaching, it has many features that are especially suitable for proficiency-oriented instruction.

Pedagogical Principles

Perhaps the most striking pedagogical principle of *Assoziationen* is the integration of the proficiency standards for the four skills developed by the American Council on the Teaching of Foreign Languages (ACTFL) in cooperation with the Educational Testing Service (ETS). All readings, cultural materials, grammar, vocabulary, and activities have been chosen or developed to give students an opportunity to practice communicative language functions in realistic situations and culturally authentic contexts. The communicative functions, or **Sprechakte** (for example, asking for and giving information, describing, comparing, agreeing, and disagreeing), are a principal focus of each lesson. Vocabulary, expressions, and structures are not ends in themselves but rather provide students with the means to perform the functions. Photographs, realia, and art support and complement these language functions and should be used by the instructor to that end.

A second key pedagogical principle of *Assoziationen* is the recycling of language functions, vocabulary, and structures. Recycling, carried throughout the textbook and even within each chapter, affords students the opportunity to refine and polish their skills at each pass. For example, the advance organizer, or **Einstimmung**, reminds students of what they already know, reviews pertinent vocabulary and structures, sets the mood, and helps establish a context for the chapter, with little new vocabulary and minimal stress.

A third pedagogical principle of *Assoziationen* is that of text- and context-based instruction, which is apparent on several levels. First, readings, activities, and exercises share a common theme within each chapter and unit. Second, they impart sociocultural information. Third, many activities are task-based or contain an informational gap; they require students to give or seek authentic, and sometimes invented, information. Thus, real communication occurs, rather than mere mechanical manipulation of structures. Contextualization and personalization of activities engages students in meaningful, purposeful, and lively language use in a way that a series of unrelated questions, fill-ins, synthetic exercises, and the like cannot do.

Readings and Reading Strategies

Novels, radio plays, short stories, magazine and newspaper articles, advertisements, polls, interviews, letters, and poetry are among the many literary and nonliterary genres represented in *Assoziationen*. Chosen to reflect a broad range of views and attitudes, the literary readings are by widely known authors and poets like Christa Wolf, Heinrich Heine, Klaus Mann, and Reiner Kunze, as well as by less well-known contemporary and sometimes unconventional writers like Yüksel Pazarkaya, Reinhardt Jung, and Wolfgang Körner. Prereading and postreading activities help students not only to get through the readings but also to appreciate their literary, sociocultural, and historical value. While constituting the core of the textbook, the readings act as a springboard for communicative activities that involve students in discussions of pertinent personal, social, cultural, political and historical issues.

All readings are preceded and followed by reading strategies, one of the special features of *Assoziationen*. Aimed at developing and sharpening reading skills, the strategies show students how to use the linguistic and cultural context to gain a global understanding of the text. The **Vor dem Lesen** and **Nach dem Lesen** sections introduce, explain, and practice reading strategies used by native readers. Since excessive glossing encourages word-by-word decoding and impedes the development of natural reading habits, vocabulary glosses appear only where they are essential to a global understanding of the text. New vocabulary is integrated and practiced in the prereading and postreading exercises. From global understanding, the students proceed to a more detailed analysis of the text, often followed by a creative or affective activity. Guided intensive reading is limited to a small number of texts.

Writing and Writing Strategies

Assoziationen also focuses systematically on improving writing proficiency. Writing opportunities are found in the **Nach dem Lesen** section, the **Aktivitäten**, and in the *Arbeitsbuch*. Strategies presented in the textbook encourage brainstorming for ideas, coherent organization, and paragraphing. Varying in detail, the *Arbeitsbuch* writing strategies section, **Vor dem Schreiben,** provides frequent step-by-step guidelines to help students improve their writing skills and make their writing interesting and persuasive.

Implementing Small Group Activities

The **Aktivitäten** in *Assoziationen* lead students from controlled and guided to more open-ended communicative tasks. With an emphasis on relevance and utility, all activities occur in a realistic, functional context. Many require students to talk or write about topics of interest to them. To maximize the time spent on communicative activities, the structural exercises have been placed in the *Arbeitsbuch*. In contrast, the textbook focuses exclusively on purposeful interpersonal communication.

Communicative activities play a key role in proficiency-oriented instruction. Small-group work promotes a noncompetitive environment and lower anxiety and stress levels, which contribute to students' progress. It also ensures that everyone has an opportunity to develop new skills and to practice those already learned, such as asking and answering questions, narrating and describing, and expressing opinions, among others. Small-group work maximizes the opportunities for speaking and listening and creates an atmosphere that fosters development of proficiency. After having worked several times in small groups, students will become more comfortable and gain confidence. Finally, small-group activities greatly expand the time each student has to speak.

Small-group activities consist of three phases. In the first phase, you should prepare students by providing a context or a model, by doing part of the activity with them, and by making sure that students understand what you expect from them. Tell them, for example, that they are to speak only in German. Encourage them to "think in German" as much as possible, by drawing on what they already know, rather than constantly asking for additional vocabulary or structures. Do not let the question, **Wie sagt man _____ auf deutsch?** become a crutch or an impediment. All students should participate in the conversations, speaking as naturally as possible. Set a time limit for the activity: three to five minutes is usually sufficient. Finally, tell students to keep notes of what they find out from their partner or their group. In this way, students will understand that they will be held accountable for what they do in the group.

During the second phase, as students work in groups, you should circulate around the room, answering questions, providing vocabulary if necessary, and insuring that students remain on task. It is advisable to have students switch partners for different activities. Be imaginative in determining how partners are chosen. In addition to the usual **Suchen Sie einen Partner . . . ,** you might assign partners or use a random "count-off" method. As a closure to the activity, allow time for accountability. In this third phase, ask students about the information they have have gathered and have a few groups report their findings to the class or perform a dialogue.

Working with Dialogues

As a model for spoken language, dialogues can provide students with an invaluable opportunity for listening comprehension by helping them build their stock of patterns, routines, set phrases, and sentences. Moreover, through dialogues students can develop a feel for word boundaries, pronunciation, and intonation. The following five steps outline an approach for presenting dialogues in which students gain both a global and a detailed understanding of the spoken texts.

1. Set the scene and establish the context of the dialogue by telling your students who is speaking, where the speakers are, and what the topic of their conversation is.

2. *Before* the first reading, ask three or four questions to focus your students' attention on the dialogue. Through focusing on key information, prelistening questions organize the text and help to establish global understanding. Since most students will be able to answer most of the questions, they will also gain a sense of achievement.
3. Read the dialogue or play it from a recording. If reading, vary your posture or use a puppet, a picture, or even a toy animal to signal the change of speaker.
4. Now ask your students to answer the questions posed to them before you read the dialogue. With longer dialogues, ask three or four questions before the first reading and another three or four questions before the second reading. Read the dialogue as often as necessary for students to answer all questions.
5. As a final step, it is often useful to ask your students to count the number of words in each sentence. This serves two purposes: First, it provides an opportunity for intensive listening by sensitizing students to listen for word boundaries and by making them notice those words that do not add much meaning (that is, "function words"). Second, it allows students to practice their receptive pronunciation. To count the words, most students repeat the sentence silently to themselves, leaving the pronunciation and intonation images crisp, clear, and undistorted by the students' as-of-yet untrained and unskilled speech organs. In addition, counting words is a gamelike activity that usually lowers the affective filter and makes students more receptive to acquisition.

After doing these listening activities, you may wish to exploit dialogues further as models for role plays. Write the three to five steps of the dialogue on the board. For example, if the dialogue models an invitation, you would outline the steps a speaker takes when inviting someone to an event:

1. **Erkundigung**
2. **Einladung**
3. **Zeit vereinbaren**
4. **sich verabschieden**

Once the steps have been outlined on the board, ask your students to provide questions and possible answers for the steps. For example:

1. **Erkundigung: Hast du heute schon was vor? Hast du morgen abend Zeit?**
2. **Einladung: Hast du Lust, ins Kino zu gehen? Wollen wir heute abend tanzen gehen?**
3. **Zeit vereinbaren: Treffen wir uns um acht vorm Kino? Wann holst du mich ab? Wann sollen wir uns treffen?**
4. **sich verabschieden: Also dann, bis heute abend. Tschüs.**

Write the (corrected) questions and answers on the board. Prepare the role play by asking students to consider and to note down personal responses to the questions. Finally, have students perform the role play in pairs.

After presenting the dialogue with the five steps outlined above, you may wish to have your students focus on grammatical forms in the dialogues. Do this only once understanding has been established—that is, once the dialogues are meaningful. For example, a dialogue in which the speakers talk about a past occurrence may be used to focus attention on past participles. Your students can write down all the participles they hear; additionally, you might have them write down the infinitive or classify the participles as weak, strong, mixed. Listening for form, after meaning has been established, draws attention to regular grammatical patterns and makes it more likely that your students will attend more frequently to these formal features and, thus, acquire them more easily.

Error Correction

While it is important to correct errors that impede communication, error correction must be done in a manner that promotes the development of proficiency. In certain types of exercises, particularly those in which new skills are introduced, you should correct errors that relate directly to the exercise. Such correction is necessary for students to master new structures and new vocabulary. However, during free-form, small-group, and skill-practicing activities, frequent correction of errors can become inhibiting. Correct only those errors that cause a breakdown in communication; let other errors pass. The focus in group activities should be on the particular language function and the ability of students to get their messages across. However, you should note patterns of error for later review and practice.

Presentation and Role of Vocabulary

The chapter end vocabulary may be considered the common core vocabulary to be learned by all students for productive purposes. Since vocabulary needs vary from class to class, you may wish to supplement the vocabulary lists with more items or even designate particular expressions for receptive understanding. Class activities and discussions provide an excellent opportunity for supplementing vocabulary in context. The *Arbeitsbuch* allows students to practice the expressions in the chapter end vocabulary as well as to reactivate their personal active vocabularies. In a proficiency-oriented approach, the testing of vocabulary should take place in contexts familiar to students. Thus, instead of rote vocabulary drills and noncontextualized vocabulary exercises, tests should be designed to give students the chance to demonstrate what they know, both by emphasizing the common core vocabulary and by offering students ample opportunity to use their personal active vocabularies. In any case, whatever your approach to vocabulary development, make your particular emphasis clear to your students.

Presentation and Role of Grammar

The grammar sections provide students with a detailed overview of German structures. Students should study each chapter carefully but should not attempt to memorize details, which are provided for their reference. In a proficiency-oriented approach, students should primarily concentrate on the functions and the meanings of German grammar, while developing an awareness of the details and integrating them gradually into their own linguistic system. In any case, make your particular emphasis on grammar clear to your students so that they can study the grammar sections accordingly.

You may wish to recommend these steps for the study of grammar to your students:

1. Read the first section carefully and jot down whatever concepts are new to you.
2. Complete the exercise(s) in the workbook that correspond to this section without referring back to the grammar explanations.
3. Check your answers against the answer key at the back of the *Arbeitsbuch* and correct them accordingly with the help of the grammar explanations.
4. Reread the same section carefully again and jot down what you think is important to remember.

At this point students should proceed to the next grammar section. In addition, you should encourage students to use the grammar sections as a reference tool for their independent writing assignments and for checking their work. The index will refer them to specific grammar topics.

The grammar sections, or **Strukturen**, in each chapter follow the same principles used by the Duden *Grammatik* (Vol. 4, 1984), in which meaning-based grammar (**inhaltbezogene Grammatik**) is combined with a valence grammar (**Valenzgrammatik**). The grammar section headings employ traditional terminology in German with which most students entering second-year German are familiar. Nevertheless, functional descriptions of these terms in English help students who may find the grammatical terms cryptic link meaning with form.

The functional descriptions emphasize the semantic and the pragmatic aspects of grammatical structures. The following grammatical explanation, taken from Chapter 13, illustrates this approach:

13.1 PASSIV 2: Passiversatz
Alternative Forms; Emphasizing the Action

A. *man*

The passive voice is used to focus on the action itself rather than on the person or the thing performing the action. Similarly, sentences with the indefinite pronoun **man** emphasize the action and deemphasize the subject.

Der neue Flughafen wird bei Erding gebaut.	*The new airport is being built near Erding.*
Man baut den neuen Flughafen bei Erding.	*They're building the new airport near Erding.*

Examples, often with their English equivalents, provide models of the structure.

Another key feature of the **Strukturen** involves the recycling of complex grammatical concepts. Broken down into smaller and more manageable bits of information, grammatical concepts are presented in order of increasing complexity over several chapters. Thus, for example, modal verbs are treated as follows:

Modalverben 1: Formen (Kapitel 2)
Modalverben 2: objektive Bedeutung (Kapitel 2)
Modalverben 3: subjektive Bedeutung (Kapitel 9)
Modalverben 4: Konjunktiv II der Vergangenheit (Kapitel 11)

Throughout the textbook, the grammar combines a review of basic structures with the introduction of more advanced points. The table of contents in the textbook and the list of grammar items below give an overview of the scope, sequence, and completeness of the grammatical syllabus of *Assoziationen*. Moreover, the index with its alphabetical listing of terminology provides students and instructors with quick and easy access to the different grammar sections.

Assoziationen is also unique in its treatment of grammatical phenomena not usually covered in first-year and even in many second-year programs. Linguistic concepts like word formation (**Wortbildung**) and text-linguistic and pragmatic items like sentence connectors (**Satzkonnektoren**) and flavoring particles (**Abtönungspartikel**) are a prominent feature of the grammar. In addition, *Assoziationen* covers all grammar points required by the *Zertifikat Deutsch als Fremdsprache* with appropriate detail. Thus, few students should have difficulty passing the grammar section of the *Zertifikat* at the end of their second year when taught with *Assoziationen*.

The grammar sections in *Assoziationen* are intended as both a grammar for reference as well as a grammar for study. Grammar exercises are therefore contained in the *Workbook/Lab manual,* where each grammar point is practiced in context. Since most of the grammar points are taken from the readings and the activities in the main text they are also used and practiced in the main text, but usually so that students are unaware that they are practicing grammar.

Grammatical knowledge is a tool that helps students to express what they want to express with accuracy. Therefore, meaningful communication should always be the primary consideration in teaching as well as in testing. Only when grammar knowledge leads to accuracy, greater ease of expression, and understanding, is it useful knowledge.

The following list of grammar topics is arranged to illustrate the order of grammar items from chapter to chapter, the frequency of their presentation, and the principle of recycling.

Kasus (Einführung)

Wortstellung 1: Überblick (Einführung)
Wortstellung 2: Objektsequenzen (1)
Wortstellung 3: Mittelfeld (9)
Wortstellung 4: Vorfeld—Thema/Rhema (13)

Adjektive 1: Adjektivendungen (1)
Adjektive 2: substantivierte Adjektive (7)

Personalpronomen (1)

Reflexiva 1: Pronomen (1)
Reflexiva 2: Zusammenfassung (12)

Interrogativa 1: Pronomen und Artikelwort (1)
Interrogativa 2: Adverbien (3)

Modalverben 1: Formen (2)
Modalverben 2: objektive Bedeutung (2)
Modalverben 3: subjektive Bedeutung (9)
Modalverben 4: Konjunktiv II der Vergangenheit (11)

wissen/kennen/können (2)

Präsens (2)

Abtönungspartikel 1: *denn* (2)
Abtönungspartikel 2: *ja, doch* (4)
Abtönungspartikel 3: *halt / eben* (7)
Abtönungspartikel 4: Imperativsätze (8)

Steigerung 1: Positiv und Komparativ (3)
Steigerung 2: Superlativ (11)
Steigerung 3: besondere Verwendung des Komparativs und Superlativs (15)

Präteritum (3)

Wortbildung 1: Komposita 1 (3)
Wortbildung 2: Komposita 2 (4)
Wortbildung 3: Derivation 1: Adjektive (8)
Wortbildung 4: Derivation 2: Verben (10)
Wortbildung 5: Derivation 3: Richtungsadverbien mit *hin* (11)
Wortbildung 6: Derivation 4: *da-, wo-, -einander, irgend-* (12)
Wortbildung 7: Konversion (15)

Perfekt (4)

Relativsätze 1: mit Relativpronomen *der, die, das* (4)
Relativsätze 2: relative Frageelemente *was, wo, wer* (6)

Satzkonnektoren 1: Konjunktoren und Subjunktoren (4)
Satzkonnektoren 2: kausale Konjunktoren und Subjunktoren, Präpositionen, Adverbien (6)
Satzkonnektoren 3: temporale Subjunktoren, Präpositionen, Adverbien (7)
Satzkonnektoren 4: finale Subjunktoren, Präpositionen und Adverbien (10)
Satzkonnektoren 5: konzessive Subjunktoren, Präpositionen, Adverbien (11)
Satzkonnektoren 6: konditionale Subjunktoren, Präpositionen, Adverbien (13)

Konjunktiv II 1 (5)
Konjunktiv II 2 (11)

Futur (5)

Plusquamperfekt (5)

als/wenn/wann (5)

Negation (5)

Schwache Maskulina (6)

Indirekte Rede 1: Konjunktiv I (6)
Indirekte Rede 2: Frage und Befehl (12)

Pronominaladverbien, *da*-Komposita (6)

Genus (6)

Possessive Adjektive und Pronomen (7)

Numerus (7)

Passiv 1: *werden*-Passiv (8)
Passiv 2: *sich lassen*, Reflexiva (13)
Passiv 3: Passiv und Stativ (15)

Aufforderung (Imperativ und andere Formen) (8)

Verbvalenz 1: Überblick (9)
Verbvalenz 2: Dativ (10)
Verbvalenz 3: Präpositionen (12)

Trennbare und untrennbare Verben (9)

Genitiv (9)

Präpositionen 1: Lage und Richtung im Raum (10)
Präpositionen 2: Akkusativ (13)
Präpositionen 3: Dativ (14)
Präpositionen 4: Genitiv (15)

stellen/stehen (10)

lassen (11)

es (12)

Partizipien 1: Präsens und Präteritum (12)
Partizipien 2: erweiterte Partizipialgruppe (14)

Konjunktiv I: Wünsche usw. (13)

da- **als Korrelat** (14)

Zeitenfolge: Vergangenheit (14)

CHAPTER NOTES

A Step-by-Step Guide to Working with Readings, Visuals, and Activities

Einführungskapitel

Opening Photo

Ask students to make associations with the photo (p. 2). If the desired response does not surface, ask more specific or leading questions or, as a last resort, yes/no questions to get at the desired associations. This should establish a context and framework for the chapter. Sample questions:

> **Wo ist das? Was ist das?**
> **Ist das ein Krankenhaus? eine Schule? eine Universität?**
> **Ist das eine deutsche oder amerikanische Schule?**
> **Wie sind die Schüler? jung? alt? Teenager?**
> **Wie kommen die Schüler zur Schule?**
> **Was steht über der Tür? Was bedeutet das?**
> **Ist diese Schule dem Körper oder dem Geist gewidmet?**

Use the photo (p. 3) in a similar fashion in the next class session.

EINSTIMMUNG: KENNENLERNEN

Drawing

Using the drawing (p. 3) to set up the interview situation.

Sample questions:

> **Wer ist das?**
> **Was machen sie?**
> **Worüber sprechen sie?**
> **Was sagt Stefan?**
> **Was sagt Julia?**

A. *Interview*

Introduce yourself to the class, then interview one student to provide a model for the activity. When you introduce yourself, include your name, office number, telephone number, and office hours. Use cognates like **Telefonnummer** and **Büronummer**. Interview the student. Sample questions:

> **Wie heißen Sie?**
> **Wo wohnen Sie?**
> **Wie ist Ihre Telefonnummer?**

B. *Vorstellen*

Introduce the student you have interviewed to the class.

Einführungskapitel

Photo

Establish a context for the reading with the photo (p. 5).

Cultural Note

(In these Cultural Notes additional background or cultural information is provided. Often in English, though occasionally in German, the note contains pertinent vocabulary needed to present the information to your class. Cultural Notes should not be photocopied or read to students verbatim. Instead, summarize the information orally when needed or desired.)

In contrast to the United States, where football and baseball are the national pastimes, Europe's most popular sport is soccer. For over 25 years (West) Germany has had a professional league, the **Bundesliga**. Players like Ray Houghton are traded across national boundaries at exorbitant sums. A sizable number of German players has joined Italian soccer clubs such as AC Milan and others. However, the players retain the right to play in the national teams of their native countries. German players, for example, are frequently called back to join the **Nationalmannschaft** before the European and World Cup championships. Both events take place every four years; the World Cup is played between the Olympiads. In the summer of 1990, Italy hosted the World Cup games, and for the first time a team from the United States participated. (West) Germany won the World Cup for the third time after World War II. In 1994 the USA will host the World Cup.

LESETEXT: DER FUSSBALLSTAR

Vor dem Lesen

A. *Was ist das Thema?*

Help students identify the logo (p. 4). Sample questions:

>   Welche Sportart ist das?
>   Was für ein Tier ist das?
>   Warum spielt der Hase Fußball?
>   Von welchem Jahr ist das Zeichen?

B. **Kognate**

Give students three minutes to skim the reading and underline all the cognates they find. Then ask them what they have found. Do not call on individual students, rather let everyone speak at once as you write the cognates they have found on the board.

C. **Was steht im Text?**

Books closed. Show a transparency of the items listed in the exercise. Have students order the items. If there are disagreements, have students vote. Then, with their books open, each student should work with a partner to verify the group's decisions. The pair activity should take no more than three minutes.

TEXT

Read the text „Houghton—Odyssee eines Stars" aloud to the class at a normal tempo. Have students read along silently. Make sure that you read each sentence with appropriate intonation and feeling. As an alternative or as a second step, have various students read lines aloud in class. Correct pronunciation and intonation.

Nach dem Lesen

Assign activities A and B as homework or have students do them in pairs or small groups as class activities.

Realia

Die Spiele der EM 1988 (p. 7). Sample questions:

> **Wann spielten die Engländer gegen die Iren?**
> **Wann fiel das Tor, in der ersten oder der zweiten Halbzeit?**
> **Wer ist erster in Gruppe I? und in Gruppe II?**
> **Wer hat das bessere Torverhältnis, BRD oder UdSSR?**

Vor dem Lesen

Do two "associograms" on the board. Sample questions:

> **Was assoziieren Sie mit dem Norden? mit dem Süden?**

LESETEXT: EIN GEDICHT

Read the poem „**Ein Fichtenbaum steht einsam**" aloud. Have students read along silently. Emphasize rhythm and texture. Read with feeling. As you read the poem a second time, have students read along in chorus. Have a few students read the poem aloud individually. Correct pronunciation and intonation.

Nach dem Lesen

A. Erkennen Sie die Wörter

Do this exercise in plenum. Help students understand the distractors without your resorting to English. As an additional activity, write the first stanza on the board, then have students read it in chorus, line for line and word for word. After each reading, remove one word or expression and have students read the poem again, supplying the missing elements. Continue until the board is empty and the students can recite the first stanza by heart. Repeat with the second stanza. Read the poem aloud again. Do not, under any circumstances, translate the poem to English. If necessary provide synonyms or circumlocutions of individual words. The poem should be understood ("felt") by the students in German.

B. Fragen zum Gedicht

Have students do No. 3 alone first, then have them work in groups of three or four on the other items. Briefly discuss what the students have discovered. You should add little or nothing to this discussion, allowing students to feel that they have discovered the essentials themselves. Allow differences of opinion to stand, without your resolving to clarifying them.

Kurzbiographie

Heinrich Heine (1797–1856): Heine ist zugleich Romantiker und Antiromantiker, Republikaner, sogar Sozialist, und Feind republikanischer Großsprecherei, Napoleonverehrer und Tyrannenhasser, promovierter Jurist und Journalist, ein Seismograph für die großen und kleinsten Erschütterungen der Zeit. Vielleicht damit wichtigster Zeuge für die dichterischen Möglichkeiten der Umbruchsperiode zwischen 1815 und 1848. Im Zentrum seines Werkes steht die Zeit- und Kulturkritik, zugleich die intensivste Vermittlung zwischen deutscher und französischer Kultur. Er schrieb Prosa („Reisebilder") und eine theoretische Abhandlung („Zur Geschichte der Religion und Philosophie in Deutschland"), aber vor allem ist er Lyriker („Buch der Lieder"). 1835 werden mit den Schriften des „Jungen Deutschland" auch Heines Bücher verboten. In dem Epos „Deutschland, ein Wintermärchen" rächt er sich für das von Deutschen erfahrene Unrecht. Warum er bis heute ein umstrittener Dichter ist, läßt sich aufgrund des Heineschen Schaffensreichtums nicht verstehen.

Picture

Use the picture of **Der Wanderer über dem Nebelmeer** (p. 9) as a point of contrast or comparison to the Heine poem. Sample questions:

> **Beschreiben Sie die Szene.**
> **Welche Wörter im Gedicht beziehen sich auch auf das Gemälde?**

Aktivitäten

Drawing

Use the family tree (p. 10) to prepare students for the following activities as well as to develop and reactivate vocabulary.

A. *Verwandte*

In groups of four or five, students should take turns asking questions of the other group members. Make it clear that their questions should be direct, such as **Wie alt ist dein Vater?** and **Wo wohnt dein Großvater?,** as opposed to the general (that is, indirect) questions given in the exercise. You may wish to initiate the exercise by asking a couple of students direct questions modeled after the indirect questions. To wrap up the activity, pose the general questions to the class.

Drawings

Use the drawings of activities (p. 11) to develop and reactivate vocabulary. Have each student describe a drawing. So that they can locate the pictures, provide them with useful expressions (for example, **oben, unten, rechts, links, in der ersten Spalte, in der dritten Reihe**). Have them use the verbs in sentences with **gern** and **nicht gern**. They should be able to say with some help:

> **In der zweiten Reihe der zweiten Spalte steht** *tanzen*.
> **Ich tanze gern, aber nicht gut.**
> **Mein Bruder tanzt nicht gern.**

Make sure all activities are mentioned. You may wish to add information or assist weaker students in stringing sentences together. This activity may be split between two class sessions.

B. *Wer tut was?*

For the first few questions, have students raise their hands to see who in the group does the various activities, then let the students work in groups of four or five to complete the poll. Poll first within the group; then, in plenum, combine polls for the entire class. Alternatively, the questions can be divided among groups to save time and provide variety. Students can also make up additional questions about other activities. Also, you might ask questions and, by a show of hands, determine "statistical" answers for the poll.

C. *Interessenprofil*

To prime students for this activity, ask students what they do in their free time. Sample questions:

> **Wer von Ihnen spielt gern Fußball?**
> **Wer liest gern Bücher?**

Then have the students do the activity in pairs and have several students report afterward to the class about their partner. Students must form questions from the infinitives given. In a second phase, tell them to make up and ask two questions with verbs that are not in the list. Then have students report to the class. In the following class session, vary this activity as a warm-up. Sample questions:

> **Erinnern Sie sich noch?**
> **Wer spielt gern Fußball?**

Drawings

Activate vocabulary with the drawings of fields of study (p. 12). Ask students about themselves (or their families, as a review of family vocabulary). Useful expressions:

Ich studiere _____.

_____ **ist mein Hauptfach/Nebenfach.**

_____ **interessiert mich (nicht).**

Ich habe _____ **gern.**

D. Stundenplan

As an additional activity or for review, have students tell their partner which areas of study they like or are good at and which areas they don't like or are not good at. (Note: The **Matura** is the Swiss and Austrian equivalent of the **Abitur**.) This activity may be done in plenum, in small groups, or as homework.

E. Feiertage erraten

This activity is a variation on "Twenty Questions." Make sure students understand what equivalent holidays are in English. Many students will not know what "Pentecost," "Epiphany," or other religious holidays are in English. Use as much German as possible in discussing this topic. Explain "double holidays" (**Ostersonntag/Ostermontag**) in Germany. You may wish to add other holidays, for example:

Aschermittwoch *Ash Wednesday*

The caption to the photo (p. 15) provides additional cultural information. Use simple etymologies and cognates to explain the German terms:

Karfreitag: kar-, *vgl. carnivore, carnal*, and so on **Fleisch**
Fronleichnam: fron-, *mask.* **zu Frau → Herr**

Here is a list of English equivalents:

Mariä Himmelfahrt	*Assumption of Maria*
Allerheiligen	*All Saints' Day*
Buß- und Bettag	*A day of prayer and repentance for Protestants*
Weihnachten	*Christmas*
Silvester, Sylvester	*New Year's Eve*
Neujahr	*New Year's Day*
Heilige Drei Könige	*Epiphany*
Karfreitag	*Good Friday*
Ostern	*Easter*
Maifeiertag	*May Day*
Christi Himmelfahrt	*Ascension Day*
Pfingsten	*Pentecost*
Fronleichnam	*Corpus Christi*
Tag der deutschen Einheit	*Day of German Unity*

Cultural Note

With the unification of Germany, the **Tag der Deutschen Einheit** (formerly June 17) is now commemorated on October 3, the day when East and West Germany were united in 1990.

Drawing

Use the drawing (p. 14) to activate vocabulary or have students review vocabulary from the drawing as homework.

F. Assoziation

Have each student go to the board in turn, draw a body part, and explain its function. Do in two parts: (1) neck and above; (2) neck and below. Sample sentences:

Das sind die Augen.	**Man sieht mit den Augen.**
Das sind die Ohren.	**Man hört mit den Ohren.** *or:*
	Man trägt Ohrringe an den Ohren.
Das ist der Mund.	**Man ißt mit dem Mund.** *or:*
	Man spricht mit dem Mund.

To complete the picture, have students first work alone for two or three minutes and then with a partner. Instructor may circulate in classroom serving as "dictionary" for students and providing cognates where possible. As an extension of this activity you may wish to play "Password": Ask students to say associated words one by one. Either a partner or the class should try to guess the respective part of the body—for example:

Hint 1: **blau**
Guess: **Leber (wrong)**

Hint 2: **Mikroskop**
Guess: **Auge (correct).**

SPRECHAKTE: *VERSTÄNDNISSICHERUNG*

Dialogues

Use first as a listening comprehension exercise. Questions to focus attention:

Dialogue 1: **Wonach fragt der Fahrgast? Was ist die Antwort?**

Note: Pronounce **rzlpflpf** as **Ritzelpflipf.**

Dialogue 2: **Wie heißt die Spezialität des Hauses? Was ist das?**

Variationen

A. Alles klar?

After students determine appropriate responses, you and a student should perform a brief role play of the situation. Afterward have students do the role play in pairs.

Realia

DJH (p. 16) stands for **Deutsche Jugendherberge.**

B. Spielen Sie!

Role plays help students polish their control of vocabulary and situational phrases. You may wish to model the situation with a proficient student first. After having students work in pairs, have several pairs perform the situations in front of the class. Then using ideas from the students' role plays, write a sample role play on the board. If time permits, allow students to do the role play again in pairs with different partners.

Cultural Note

The youth hostel movement, which originated in Germany before World War I, enables young men and women to stay overnight at inexpensive hostels. Hostels are very common in Germany and in many other European countries. West Germany alone had about 560 youth hostels. Some of them are located in beautiful places, such as in old castles overlooking the Rhine or on the border of Lake Windermere in England. In 1986, every tenth guest in a German **Jugendherberge** was a foreigner, which makes youth hostels a very good place to meet young people from other cultures and countries.

C. Zum Schluß

This activity can be employed as a restructuring exercise. Have students walk around the classroom looking for others with the given characteristics by asking questions such as **Spielst du gern Tennis?** Follow up by having a few students report to the class what they found out. Then ask general questions in plenum such as **Wer spielt gern Tennis?**, obtaining three or four answers from various students. As an alternative, prepare a handout with these activities listed and a line for a signature next to each activity. Students circulate in the class asking their questions. For each affirmative response they should get a signature. The student who has the most signatures or is the first to have all activities signed for wins.

Thema I: Spiegelbilder

Opening Photo

Ask "*wh*-questions" that stimulate creative and associative thinking about the photo (p. 23). Sample questions:

> **Wer sind diese Leute?**
> **Was machen Sie?**
> **Warum ist das ein „Spiegelbild"?**

Kapitel 1: Der Mensch im Spiegel

Opening Photo

Ask questions about the photo (p. 24). Sample questions:

> **Ist diese Person alt oder jung?**
> **Wie alt könnte sie sein?**
> **Hat die Person langes oder kurzes Haar?**
> **Was glauben Sie, geht sie oft oder selten zum Frisör?**

Afterward, you may also wish to ask questions that cannot be answered from the photo alone but rather from an image that the students have in mind. Sample questions:

> **Was glauben Sie, ist diese Person verheiratet?**
> **Hat sie Kinder?**
> **Was könnte sie von Beruf sein?**
> **Glauben Sie, daß sie glücklich in ihrem Beruf ist?**
> **Warum sieht sie in den Spiegel?**
> **Was denkt sie wohl gerade?**

This exercise aims to review vocabulary that will be useful in later activities of the unit, to provide the student with spoken German input, and to introduce new vocabulary and set the stage for the theme of the unit.

Kapitel 1

EINSTIMMUNG: WAS TRAGEN SIE?

Drawings

Use the drawings (p. 25) to reactivate vocabulary. A transparency can be made from the master in the *Visual Materials and Activities* (VMA) folder. Sample questions:

> **Was tragen diese Personen?**
> **Das ist eine Sonnenbrille. Wann trägt man eine Sonnenbrille?**
> **Das ist ein Schlafanzug. Wer von Ihnen hat keinen Schlafanzug?**
> **Das ist ein Ring. Wie viele von Ihnen tragen heute einen Ring?**

As a related exercise, pose questions that will elicit descriptions. Sample questions:

> **Beschreiben Sie mich!**
> **Bin ich groß oder klein? dick oder dünn?**
> **Wie sind meine Haare? meine Augen?**
> **Was trage ich? Welche Farbe hat/haben mein/e . . . ?**
> **Trage ich etwas an den Fingern? am Arm? am Hals? an den Ohren? an der Nase?**

Games can be easily based on this activity. Game 1: Send two students out of classroom before explaining the exercise. These should be students who do not mind being the center of attention. If possible, they should also be dressed in brightly colored or unusual clothes. Have those students remaining in the classroom describe in as much detail as possible the clothing, accessories, hair styles, and other features of the two students. List these on the board. When the students return, have the class make comparisons. Repeat two or three times. You may wish to provide guidance. Sample questions:

> **Was trägt er/sie?**
> **Welche Farbe hat/haben . . . ?**

Game 2: **Wer ist das?** Ask a student to describe the clothes, using adjectives of color and patterns, that another student is wearing. The other students should try to guess who it is. For example:

> **Ihre Schuhe sind weiß. Ihre Hose ist blau. Ihr Pullover ist braun.**

LESETEXT: EIN UNGEWÖHNLICHES MÄDCHEN

Vor dem Lesen

Have students read the introduction and write the activity **Vorhersagen machen** as homework. In the following class session, do a brief pair activity in which students compare their findings with those of a partner.

Nach dem Lesen

A. Was steht im Text?

Do this activity in plenum.

B, C, and D

These activities can be done as pair work, alone silently in class, assigned as homework, or any combination of the three. Discuss the results of C and D briefly. Answers to C:

> **pechschwarz, Lockenkopf, Fußknöchel, Männerjacke, Handgelenke, zusammenpassen, zusammennähen**

Answers to D:

> **Berührung, Ordnung, Erscheinung, Sauberkeit**

Sample follow-up questions:

> **Aus welchen Wörtern bestehen diese Komposita?**
> **Woher kommen diese Komposita?**

Though the nouns in D are actually derivatives, it is all right to refer to them as **Komposita** for purposes of this activity.

E. *Gefühlsbarometer*

Have students do this activity at first alone silently, then in groups of three. To explain the activity, say:

> **Vergleichen Sie Ihre Antworten. Wenn alle drei die gleiche haben, machen Sie ein Kreuz vor das Adjektiv.**
> **Lesen Sie die Adjektive der Reihe nach vor. Nur wenn alle drei sagen, daß das eine sehr wichtige Eigenschaft ist, machen Sie einen Kreis vor das Adjektiv.**

During this group activity, you should circulate to make sure that everything is clearly understood, to provide needed additional vocabulary, and to insure that all students remain on task. As a follow-up in plenum, write Momo's characteristics on the board, as well as those adjectives that were felt to be very important. In conclusion, have a brief discussion. Sample questions:

> **Wer hätte Momo gern zur Freundin? Warum?**

Aktivitäten

Drawing

Use the drawing of the zodiac (p. 29, also in *VMA*) to develop students' working knowledge of the signs of the zodiac and their animal symbols; call attention to the relationship between sign and symbol and to the relationship between German and English—for example, **Krebs** = *crab*, **Krebs** = *cancer*.

Cultural Note

Even more so than in the United States, horoscopes fill the pages of all but the top newspapers in Germany. Daily predictions are of the familiar type (**Sie können heute in geldlichen Angelegenheiten Erfolg haben; Sie sollten heute keine große Reise antreten**). While few people actually heed them, many nonetheless turn to the horoscope page just to see what it says. With the exception of *Der Spiegel* and special-interest or professional (weekly) magazines, virtually all German periodicals carry horoscopes. All radio and TV program magazines carry horoscopes and frequently feature a famous personality.

B. *Interaktion*

This activity aims to encourage free interaction among students and to reduce inhibition in speaking German. In preparation for this activity (perhaps in a prior session), have students line up according to age and ask each other **Wie alt bist du?** To begin the activity, have the students line up across the room according to the signs of the zodiac, starting with Aries (**Widder**). Tell students that they are to ask one another questions to determine their respective positions in line. Model sample questions for the students as in the example.

C. *Selbstanalyse*

Have students draw a grid with three columns on a piece of paper (put a model on the chalkboard). Each column is given a heading: **Wie ich bin, Wie ich nicht bin,** and **Wie ich gern sein möchte.** Give students three minutes to write five words per column about themselves, using vocabulary from the list. Encourage students to be playful, perhaps by exaggerating their real character traits. Use the next exercise as a follow-up to this activity.

Kapitel 1

D. Interview

Conceived as a partner activity, this exercise should encourage "natural" responses. As a follow-up, have students connect a specific student with a specific characteristic, based on the interviews. Ask questions in plenum. Sample questions:

>**Karen, wie heißt Ihr Nachbar, und wie ist er? —Er heißt Bob, und er ist emanzipiert und sensibel.**

After five or six students have done this, ask more questions to jog their memories. Sample questions:

>**Erinnern Sie sich noch?**
>**Wie war Bob?**

Allow only positive characteristics to be used here.

SPRECHAKTE: *BESCHREIBEN*

The model text provides an example of useful vocabulary and structures. Use the text as a listening comprehension activity. Before reading the text, put the following grid on the board:

Students should take notes while you read the dialogue. After the first reading elicit the information requested. If students have not understood everything, read the dialogue again.

Variationen

Have students perform the role play several times through, eventually without books. Assign the second and third items as homework, or do them as a quick in-class individual or group activity. In the next session as a review, have students give descriptions orally without referring to their written work.

LESETEXT: IM TREND

Cultural Note

Of all German magazines, *Stern* has the highest weekly circulation. Some 35 or 40 years ago, its layout was similar to that of *Life* magazine. Since then, however, it has developed into a somewhat odd collection of serious reporting and, at times, racy photography. Feature stories in *Stern* have ranged from a beautiful, 45-page photo essay on the United States to the copyrighted advance publication of Adolf Hitler's diaries, which, it turned out, were forgeries. A typical isssue of *Stern* might carry interviews with one of the world's most famous—or infamous—politicians, chastise a flaw in the German social or legal system in a short *Spiegel*-style article, and feature a 30-page cover story (with a cover photo of a topless bathing beauty) on this summer's most desirable beaches.

Vor dem Lesen

A. *Vorher und hinterher*

Working with a partner, students should describe Matthias Matussek in the photos (pp. 33, 35). Ask students what features have been changed. For a brief follow-up, write two composite lists on the board.

B. *Definitionen*

Have students do this activity in groups of three or four. Give them a tip. Sample explanation:

> Sie sollen das auslassen, was Sie nicht wissen. Später kommen Sie darauf zurück, wenn weniger Alternativen da sind. Denken Sie auch daran, daß ein Nomen durch ein anderes Nomen, ein Verb durch ein anderes Verb ersetzt wird. Sie sollen auch den Kontext mit einbeziehen!

Afterward, check the results with students in plenum.

C. *Wie man Zeitungs- oder Zeitschriftentexte liest*

Have students read the introduction to reading strategies silently and the questions to **Teil 1.** Then have them work with a partner to answer the questions. Review their answers briefly in plenum. Assign **Teil 2** and **Teil 3** as homework. Sample explanation:

> Bitte, erinnern Sie sich daran, daß Sie genug vom Text verstanden haben, wenn sie die Fragen beantwortet haben. Mehrmaliges Lesen bringt mehr als Wörter nachzuschlagen. Sie sollen diesen Text auf keinen Fall intensiv lesen, d.h., lesen Sie den Text nicht Wort für Wort!

Nach dem Lesen

A. „Wortfarben"

Assign as homework or, if time permits, do as pair work in class. Do a brief wrap-up in class.

Cultural Note

The **Alternativbewegung** of the 1970s and 1980s is a movement not limited to Germany. Mostly a loose grouping of young people opposing the dominant political, social, and cultural order, it became a well-organized movement in (West) Berlin that began putting up candidates for the city government in 1979. The **Alternative Liste** (or **AL**) managed to garner 7.5% of the popular vote in 1981, which allowed it to seat nine deputies for the first time. The **AL** has been a political force in (West) Berlin ever since. Its deputies frequently stood in total opposition to the governing majority party.

Aktivitäten

A. *Interview*

As a follow-up or alternative, have students think of a person they know and jot down a number of his or her characteristics. Then, as a partner activity, have them describe to their partner the person they thought of. Finally, have several students describe their persons in plenum.

B. *Umfrage*

In this recombination activity, students circulate in the classroom and ask questions looking for affirmative answers. Those that answer with **Ja** sign the blank next to the question they answered affirmatively. No student should sign more than twice for the same student.

SPRECHAKTE: *BERATEN*

Use as a listening comprehension exercise with books closed. Before the first reading, ask these questions to focus students' attention:

> Dialogue 1: **Wohin möchte Fritz gehen? Was soll er anziehen? Wohin soll Fritz nach Meinung seiner Schwester gehen?**
> Dialogue 2: **Woher kommt das Heimtrainingsgerät? Welche Muskeln können damit trainiert werden? Woraus besteht die Gebrauchsanweisung?**

Extend the questions beyond the dialogue (for example, **Woher kommt Arnold Schwarzenegger?**)

Realia

Use the Polysoft realia (p. 37) to illustrate how the English language pervades the German, especially in advertisements. Have students make a list of all English loan words in the ad (**polysoft, finishing, styling, -spray, form**). In a second list add words which have been borrowed and "Germanized" (**Haarspray, Stylen**). A third list might contain English-German cognates (**Haar, Volumen, perfekt, Elastizität, individuell, Varianten**). As a related assignment, have students write an ad of their own for homework or together in class with a partner.

Variationen

A. *Cartoon*

Have students work in groups. Encourage dialogues that fit the cartoon and have one figure offering advice to the other. Compare dialogues in plenum. Check for accuracy of structure and vocabulary.

UND JETZT ZU IHNEN!

These role plays are slightly more complicated and open-ended than those in **Sprechakte** sections. Encourage students to prepare and practice them at home. In the first chapters you may wish to give students three or four minutes with a partner to rehearse these role plays in class before performing them in plenum. The role plays work best if they have been photocopied and affixed to index cards. Ask two students to improvise the role play in front of the class. A travel poster for Austria can support and encourage students. Have the remainder of the class track the role play. Sample instructions:

> **Welche Fragen werden gestellt? Was sind die Antworten? Machen Sie sich Notizen.**

Afterwards ask:

> **Also, was waren die Fragen? Und was waren die Antworten? Welche anderen Fragen könnte man stellen? Und was wären hier mögliche Antworten?**

As students respond, write the corrected questions and answers on the board. Then have the whole class work in pairs to role-play these situations.

Kapitel 2: Schau mir in die Augen

Opening Photo

Have students brainstorm about the situation in the photo to establish a context for the chapter and to elicit useful vocabulary.

EINSTIMMUNG: LIEBE, EHE, PARTNERSCHAFT

As an initial activity, have students raise their hands in response to the following questions:

> **Wie viele von Ihnen ...**
> **sind verheiratet? wie lange schon?**
> **sind ledig?**
> **haben Kinder? wie viele?**
> **haben keine Kinder?**
> **wollen heiraten?**
> **wollen nicht heiraten?**
> **wollen Kinder?**
> **wollen keine Kinder?**

Chart student interests in marriage and children on the board. As a second activity, do an associogram for the word **Partner** on the board. Write **PARTNER** in the center of an imaginary wheel, draw radiating lines as "spokes," and write the words the students associate with the key word on the spokes. As a third activity, list student responses to the following questions on the board:

> **Welche Charaktereigenschaften sollte der ideale Partner haben?** (list about six characteristics)
> **Wie sollte er oder sie sein?**
> **Welche von diesen Eigenschaften finden Sie am wichtigsten?** (prioritize the characteristics)

Gruppenarbeit

Read the list of adjectives with the class to insure proper pronunciation and understanding. After students do the activity, have the groups report in plenum about the results. Compile a chart on the board.

LESETEXT: DER TYP, DER MIR GEFÄLLT

In preparation for the reading, brainstorm with the class. Sample questions:

> **Was denken junge Deutsche?**
> **Wie stellen sie sich den idealen Partner vor?**
> **In dem Text kommen drei junge Deutsche zu Wort.**

Have students look at the text, and ask:

> **Wie heißen die drei jungen Leute?**
> **Wie alt sind sie?**
> **Was glauben Sie, wie stellen sich diese drei ihren idealen Partner vor?**

Vor dem Lesen

Vorhersagen

You may wish to mention that this is a scanning activity. Students should look for specific pieces of information by scanning the text quickly without reading it in detail. Have students read the activity silently alone and make notes for themselves as answers to the questions. Then have them skim the reading to check their answers. Do a brief wrap-up.

Nach dem Lesen

Do exercises A and B in groups of three. Have students find the corresponding points in the text by scanning. Do a brief wrap-up. Do exercise C in groups of three or four. Then ask:

> Was sind die Eigenschaften, die Gabi, Armin und Steffi sich bei ihren Partnern/Partnerinnen wünschen?
> Finden Sie diese Eigenschaften wichtig?
> Welche Eigenschaften finden Sie wichtig?

This activity may also be done as a homework assignment.

Aktivitäten

A. Wo findet man am besten einen Ehepartner/eine Ehepartnerin?

This activity may be done in groups of three, in plenum, individually in class, or at home in preparation for class. As a wrap-up, ask questions to find out whether any of the students have indeed found a partner in one of the locations mentioned. Sample questions:

> Hat jemand einen Partner oder eine Partnerin beim Frisör kennengelernt?
> Lernt jemand Deutsch, um einen Partner zu finden?

B. Wie sucht man am besten einen Partner/eine Partnerin?

As a wrap-up to this activity, poll students to rank the options from most to least likely. List results on the board.

Cultural Note

Although ads for companionship can be found in the "Personals" of most American newspapers, few marriages or permanent relationships actually result from such ads. However, in Germany and in many other European countries one or more pages of the Saturday (that is, weekend) edition of all newspapers may be filled with **Heiratsanzeigen, Ehewünschen,** or simply **WM (weiblich/männlich),** as the section may be titled. As if to underline the seriousness of these advertisements, papers like the *Frankfurter Allgemeine Zeitung* or the *Süddeutsche Zeitung* often differentiate between **Heiratsanzeigen** (subdivided in **männlich** and **weiblich,** or **Herren/Damen**), **Bekanntschaften,** and the often more ephemeral **Reisebekanntschaften.** Major newspapers generally do not carry so-called **Kontaktanzeigen.** This category is found in many alternative papers. Its ads are often used to establish acquaintanceships.

Young people may resort to finding a partner through ads, stating somewhat apologetically: **Durch langes Studium verhindert, mich um eine Partnerin zu kümmern, suche ich auf diesem Weg . . .** Indeed, parents advertise for their children (and vice versa) and friends on behalf of their **Freund** or **Freundin.** In papers with nationwide distribution, German emigrants to the United States or South America may initiate a partner search in hopes of finding someone to join them abroad: **Jetzt, da ich in Florida ein Vermögen erworben habe, . . .** Such advertisements rely much less on abbreviations than the WM-type ads, which frequently pack information into two lines.

Realia

„Lonely Hearts," the WM column (p. 55), a take-off on the common abbreviation for **(Fußball) Weltmeisterschaft**—presumably the people placing these ads are champions—combines three types of advertisements: **Heiratsanzeigen, Bekanntschaften,** and **Reisebekanntschaften.** These particular ads, from the Hamburg weekly newspaper *Die Zeit,* have been placed by persons in their late thirties or older. Have students talk in small groups about the various people listed in the ads. Which prospects are most promising? Why? Who is desperate? Whom do your students find particularly attractive?

C. Wie sieht Ihr idealer Partner/Ihre ideale Partnerin aus?

You may wish to refer students back to the **Einführungskapitel** for vocabulary. This is a good opportunity to reenter and recycle vocabulary fields. The drawing (p. 56, top) may also provide further examples and vocabulary.

SPRECHAKTE: *SICH VORSTELLEN*

Review these ads (p. 56) in the same manner as the realia (p. 55). To introduce the ads, you might say:

> **In fast allen deutschen Zeitungen finden sich Heiratsanzeigen. Leute jeden Alters und sozialer Stellung schreiben solche Anzeigen, und viele Paare haben sich auf diese Weise gefunden.**

Variationen

B. Spielen Sie!

As a follow-up, have various groups read their ads aloud. Poll the class to find out which persons they find most attractive or most striking. As a homework assignment, you may wish to ask students to respond to the ad they find most interesting.

LESETEXT: DIE ANNÄHERUNG

Assign the text (from *Der geteilte Himmel*) as homework. Have students read **Vor dem Lesen** and **Nach dem Lesen: Textsalat** as well. You might tell students:

> **Bitte diesen Text nicht zu intensiv lesen! Benutzen Sie ein Wörterbuch nur, wenn der Kontext nicht weiterhilft und wenn die Textstellle, das Wort oder der Ausdruck unbedingt wichtig für die zu lösende Aufgabe sind!**

As an alternative, have students read the English introduction silently in class and make notes for themselves. Then do **Vor dem Lesen** and **Nach dem Lesen**: Textsalat as pair work. Do a brief wrap-up.

A. Was trifft wohl zu?

Do as pair work or as homework.

D. Beschreibender Erzählstil

First question: You may wish to ask students to work alone and underline these words and expressions in the text. Then, in plenum, write them on the board. For the second question, which may also be used as a writing activity, you may wish to ask the students which characteristics they find more positive or more negative. Ask what their overall subjective impression of Manfred is. In addition, you may wish to follow up with questions such as:

> **Würden Sie Manfred gern kennenlernen?**
> **Worüber könnten Sie sich mit ihm unterhalten?**

Finally, you may wish to review the two most common types of narration: first person and third person.

LESETEXT: LYRIK

Nach dem Lesen

To stimulate students' imagination and as a transition to the group activity that follows, you may wish to work with free associations. Write the poem on the board, one line at a time. For each line, elicit from the students associated words and phrases. For example, for the first line students may provide words such as

häßlich (opposite), **hübsch** (synonym), **Wetter** or **Landschaft** (associated nouns), **schreiben** or **aussehen** (associated verbs), and so on. After a few associations, move on to the next line. As the poem progresses, the field of choices narrows and the focus of the poem becomes more apparent.

Gruppenarbeit

Note on question No. 4: An acoustical opposition occurs between the two stanzas and emphasizes the transition from **langsam** to **schnell**. In the first stanza, make long pauses between the words, since each word is, for all practical purposes, a line by itself. Note the many dark and therefore **langsam** vowels. In the second stanza, there are hardly any pauses, and the vowels are "front" and "forward" in the mouth. You may have your students write a poem alone at home. As a variation, students may write poems in small groups or create them as a chain activity in which each student in turn adds a line. In this case, you may wish to provide the title or the first line.

Cultural Note

In many European countries, especially in Switzerland, Austria, and Germany, a great number of trades and professions require several years of training or apprenticeship and certification. In Germany, there are about 400 officially defined and accredited trades, professions, or vocations. Sixty percent of men and seventy-five percent of women want to become automobile mechanics, electricians, painters, carpenters, hairdressers, salespersons, or medical technicians. These are among the twenty most preferred vocations. In all cases, practical training takes place at the workplace. For a period of three years an apprentice must attend a **Berufsschule** for one or even two days a week, where he/she receives further practical and theoretical training in the area of specialization and in subjects like sociology or political science. After three years as a **Lehrling** (*apprentice*)—or, to use the newly created official term, **Auszubildender** (literally, *someone to be trained*, abbreviated **Azubi**—an apprentice has to take the **Gesellenprüfung** (*journeyman's examination*), which establishes him/her in the profession. A number of **Gesellen** will continue in their training and, after having gathered further practical experience, will attend highly specialized and advanced trade schools that are frequently found only in one location in the country. Bakers can become **Bäckermeister**, butchers **Metzger-** (*or* **Fleischermeister**, and painters **Malermeister**. Only masters of their trades are allowed to apprentice young people. Such establishments frequently, and proudly, advertise that they are a **handwerklicher Ausbildungsbetrieb** providing vocational training. This well-established vocational training system has its roots in the Middle Ages, when the guilds first established rigid guidelines for the training of their apprentices. Only after World War II did (West) Germany adopt the American system of free and open trades (**Berufsfreiheit**). Up to then, only masters of their trades could open shops. Today, anyone may promote himself/herself as a house painter but not as a **Malermeister**.

Aktivitäten

A. **Was meinen Sie?**

Read through the list of occupations with students to insure proper pronunciation and understanding. Before doing this activity, you might ask:

> **Was sind Ihre Eltern von Beruf?**
> **Welcher Beruf hat am meisten Prestige?**   (write one or two on the board)

As an alternative, have students work in groups of three to compare, line for line, which of the two occupations on that line has the most prestige.

B. **Was ist Ihnen wichtig?**

Briefly discuss the list of characteristics. Give students two or three minutes to mark four items that are important to them. Have students add other categories to the list. Reinforce the appropriate question form here. Possible approach:

> **Wie stellt man diese Fragen?**
> **Angenommen Sie suchen jetzt in dieser Klasse den idealen Partner, wie würden Sie fragen?**

Follow-up in plenum:

> **Wie viele von Ihnen halten die politische Einstellung eines Partners für sehr wichtig?**

SPRECHAKTE: *EINLADEN/SICH VERABREDEN*

Use first as a listening comprehension exercise. Ask questions to focus students' attention:

> **Wohin wollen Rainer und Hanni?**
> **Was gibt es da?**
> **Wann wollen sie los?**
> **Kommt Werner mit?**

After the context of the dialogue has been clearly established, use the dialogue as a starting point for role-playing. Ask:

> **Wie lädt man ein?**
> **Was sagt man, wenn man sich verabreden möchte?**
> **Was sagt man, wenn man eine Einladung annimmt?**
> **Was sagt man, wenn man sie ablehnt?**

Write a few responses, in their corrected form, on the board. Finally, ask students to name an event to which they might like to invite someone. Have them perform a quick role play (ca. 1–2 minutes).

Variationen

Before beginning, discuss the elements of an invitation. Sample approach:

> **Eine Einladung besteht oft aus vier Teilen:**
> 1. **Erkundigung: Hast du heute schon was vor? Hast du morgen abend Zeit?**
> 2. **Einladung: Hast du Lust, ins Kino zu gehen? Wollen wir heute abend tanzen gehen?**
> 3. **Zeit vereinbaren: Treffen wir uns um acht vorm Kino. Wann holst du mich ab? Wann sollen wir uns treffen?**
> 4. **sich verabschieden: Also dann bis heute abend. Tschüß.**

Spielen Sie!

First have students make a schedule of their (imaginary) activities for the week. On three evenings they plan activities; on four evenings they remain free. Do a recombination activity in which students try to find other students who wish to participate in the three activities they have planned. Have them write down names of potential participants. They can use their free evenings to participate in activities proposed by others. When they accept another student's invitation, they should write that student's name and the activity on their schedule. As an alternative, divide the class into two equal groups. One group writes down possible invitations and how to make them, the other group writes down how to accept or reject invitations. Each student gets a partner from the other group and then does activity No. 1. Follow up with questions. Sample questions:

> **Wessen Einladungen wurden angenommen?**
> **Wozu wurde eingeladen?**

Next, write a model conversation on the board to prepare the students for the role play.

Kapitel 3: Rollenspiele

Opening Photos

To introduce the chapter theme, work with the photos (p. 78). Sample questions:

> Was ist er/sie von Beruf?
> Ist das normal?
> Ist das typisch?
> Ist das gut?
> Wären Sie gern Pilot/Pilotin? Koch/Köchin?

EINSTIMMUNG: TYPISCH MÄNNLICH/TYPISCH WEIBLICH?

As an initial activity, brainstorm with the students. Write a list of ideas on the board, or use an associogram for **Mann** and **Frau**. Sample questions:

> Was assoziieren Sie mit *Mann*? mit *Frau*?
> Welche Berufe üben Männer aus?
> Welche Berufe üben Frauen aus?

Go through the lists on the board and ask:

> Was sind eher Klischees, was ist eher Realität?

Cultural Note

Owing to the shortage of young men in the former GDR, women embarked on careers that were long considered "male occupations." Women truck drivers, crane operators, automobile mechanics, and bricklayers were a common sight in the GDR many years before women began to make inroads in these professions in the West. The GDR had one of the highest percentages of female doctors in the world. Despite all this, very few women managed to climb up to the higher levels of the party (**SED**), the government, or managerial positions.

Drawings

The drawings (p. 79) lend themselves to a discussion of "cross-over" professions, typical male-female roles, and changing roles, among other things.

A. *Was meinen Sie?*

Read through the list of adjectives in class to familiarize the students with the vocabulary. Pictures (such as of a mother and her baby to illustrate *zärtlich*), gestures (mimic a shy person to illustrate *bescheiden*), and short definitions in German (**sehr genau, exakt** for *präzise*) help students access the vocabulary. Allow students time to work alone on the exercise before they form groups. Ideally, the groups should have a balance of males and females. Sample follow-up questions:

> Bei welchen Adjektiven haben alle in der Gruppe dasselbe eingetragen?

LESETEXT: ADAM UND EVA

Cultural Note

Holger Börner (SPD) war von 1984–1987 Ministerpräsident von Hessen. Er versuchte als erster SPD-Politiker mit den Grünen zusammenzuarbeiten und ernannte einen Grünen zum Umweltminister.

Vor dem Lesen

Emanzipiert oder traditionell?

Have students work silently and make notes. The main objective is for students to look at the pictures and get a general impression of these people. Briefly collect answers to the questions; go into greater detail on points of interest.

TEXT

Give students about two minutes to read the text („**Worte der Woche**") under the photos.

Nach dem Lesen

A. Wer sagt was?

Have students work in groups of three. Give a tip such as:

> **Wählen Sie zuerst die offensichtlichen Entsprechungen und haken Sie sie ab; lesen Sie dann die Texte noch einmal dort, wo es Probleme gibt.**

Have students briefly report their results in plenum.

B. Talk-Show

As an alternative, collect the names of prominent people on the board. Students should write down their ideas about what such people would say about male and female roles for homework. In the class session, each student can then play the role of the prominent personality he or she has chosen and be interviewed by other students.

LESETEXT: ROLLENSPIELE

Cultural Note

The **Hörspiel** (*radio play*), while very popular in the United States from the 1920s to the end of World War II (you may be familiar with Orson Welles' 1938 "War of the Worlds" scare on CBS), saw its demise in this country with the advent of television. In the German-speaking countries, the belated introduction of television and the system of state-owned radio stations meant that the radio play as the most original medium of the airwaves has remained an important art form to this very day. Almost every station has a **Hörspiel-Studio** that broadcasts **Kriminalhörspiele** (*mystery radio plays*) or **Experimentelle Hörspiele**, the latter relying heavily on the acoustic properties of the radio. Radio stations continue to commission new plays, and, since 1951, the **Bund der Kriegsblinden Deutschlands** (*Association of Blind War Veterans*) has annually awarded the coveted **Hörspielpreis der Kriegsblinden** to well-known postwar authors like Günther Eich. Influential works like Wolfgang Borchert's "Draußen vor der Tür" (1947) were first made available as radio plays before being performed on stage.

Vor dem Lesen

Teile benennen und Sprecher identifizieren

This activity requires advance preparation. Allow fifteen minutes for this activity. Divide the class into eight groups. Each group should read one section of the text. Since the sections vary in difficulty and length make sure that the best-prepared groups take on the more difficult texts. The level of difficulty is marked below in parentheses: 1 = **leicht**; 2 = **mittel**; 3 = **schwer**. Since vocabulary help is purposely not given until the **Nach dem Lesen** activities, you may need to provide some additional help here.

> **Gruppe 1:** Zeile 1–7 (1)
> **Gruppe 2:** Zeile 8–20 (2)
> **Gruppe 3:** Zeile 21–34 (2)
> **Gruppe 4:** Zeile 35–50 (3)
> **Gruppe 5:** Zeile 51–63 (2)
> **Gruppe 6:** Zeile 64–88 (1)
> **Gruppe 7:** Zeile 89–106 (2)
> **Gruppe 8:** Zeile 107–122 (3)

Have the groups report their findings in plenum. Use a random order of groups, not a chronological order. Allow students to make notes in preparation for the next step. Give students fifteen minutes to "put the pieces together." List the "titles" chosen by students on the board. Establish the correct sequence in plenum.

Cultural Note

A **Stammtisch** is reserved for regular patrons of a bar or restaurant. It is usually marked accordingly, and other guests are not permitted to sit down there. **Stammtischgespräche** range from local gossip to national politics, and many a friendship has ended after such a heated discussion.

Cultural Note

Carl Orff (1895–1982) developed a school for gymnastics, rhythmics, and expressive dance in the 1920s, where he developed his music pedagogy and along with it a new group of rhythmic instruments. The result was the **Orffsche Schulwerk** (1930–1935), in which he stressed rhythmic elements and percussion instruments. In Germany and Austria, entire generations of children have been trained in this method; since 1963, a special institute attached to the **Salzburg Mozarteum** has been preparing music teachers in Orff's method. Although the **Orffsche Schulwerk** is hardly known in the United States, Orff's resetting of *Carmina Burana*, late medieval songs that he unearthed in a Bavarian monastery, can be heard frequently in this country.

Nach dem Lesen

A, B, and C can be done as homework or as pair work.

C. Ratschläge

Compare the English proverb:

> **"A whistling girl and a cackling hen will always come to some bad end."**

and the response:

> **"Whistling girls and a band of sheep are the very best flock a man can keep."**

Let students speculate on the origin of such proverbs.

D. Interaktion

Have students read the parts of the play, à la reader's theater, very theatrically and with feeling. As an alternative, you may wish to tape part of the radio play in a subsequent class session so that the students have time to rehearse their parts.

Aktivitäten

A. *Was ist Ihre Meinung?*

Give students a few minutes to mark several clichés for themselves, then have them work in groups to arrive at a composite list. Guide the comparison of lists with the class in plenum. Write composite lists on the board.

B. *Was meinen Sie?*

Here again guide the discussion by putting lists on the board. Elicit responses from many students, moving quickly from one situation to another and listing as many responses as possible. List occupations and situations as a point of departure for the group activity.

SPRECHAKTE: IDENTITÄT UND ENTSPRECHUNG

First read the minidialogues aloud as a listening comprehension activity for the class. Before each dialogue, ask questions such as:

Dialogue 1: **Wohin möchte Dieter? Warum geht Susan nicht mit?**
Dialogue 2: **Was sucht die Mutter? Was sagt der Vater?**
Dialogue 3: **Wohin möchte der Kunde? Wann? Wohin gibt es eine Tour?**

Using the three minidialogues as a basis, work out a generic model for this type of interview with the students. Ask, for example:

Welche Fragen werden gestellt?
Was sind die Antworten?

List the responses on the board. Have several student pairs role-play the minidialogues.

Cartoon

Use the cartoon (p. 88) to point out the difference between *dasselbe* and *das gleiche*. Students should use intuition and reasoning to deduce the difference.

Variationen

Spielen Sie!

Divide the class into groups and distribute the situations among the groups. Have a couple of the groups present their situations in plenum.

LESETEXT: DORNRÖSCHEN

Cultural Note

Josef Reding's version of „**Dornröschen**" ("*Sleeping Beauty*") is a modernized version and parody of the fairy tale first collected and published by the Brothers Grimm in their ***Kinder- und Hausmärchen*** of 1812–1822.

Vor dem Lesen

As an introduction, have students recall as a group a fairy tale such as "Snow White" or "Cinderella."

Cartoon

With the help of the cartoon (p. 89), talk about German fairy tales. Mention the introductory line **Es war einmal ...** and compare it with its English equivalent. Which fairy tale does the cartoon remind students of? What is the effect of **ich bin ein Prinz und suche eine Frau**? How does that expression differ from **ich bin der Prinz und suche die Frau (, der dieser Schuh paßt)**?

Erzählen Sie

Have students work in groups to establish the correct sequence.

TEXT

Read the poem „**Mädchen, pfeif auf den Prinzen**" aloud, allowing students to read along silently.

Discuss briefly, in German, the content of the poem. Sample questions:

1. Strophe: Was soll das Mädchen nicht machen?
2. Strophe: Was soll das Mädchen machen?
3. Strophe: Was macht der Prinz nicht?
4. Strophe: Was soll das Mädchen machen?

Note: Der Gebrauch von *Mädchen/es* wirkt mittlerweile sexistisch. Das *Mädchen/sie* setzt sich mehr und mehr durch, obwohl offiziell *sie* nur verwendet werden darf, wenn das Mädchen mit Vornamen näher bezeichnet wird. Also *das Mädchen/es*, aber *Das Mädchen da drüben heißt Elke. Sie ist schon sieben.*

Nach dem Lesen

A. *Fragen zum Gedicht*

Assign as homework.

C. *Schreiben Sie ein Märchen!*

In preparation for this activity, work out a generic structure for a fairy tale with your students. Place and time are unimportant, but you will need a hero or heroine (*-r Held, -e Heldin*), a villain (*-r Bösewicht*), and a champion/savior (*-r Retter, -e Retterin*). Typical fairy tale figures (p. 91) should be complemented by additional vocabulary such as: *verfluchen, verwünschen, erlösen, verzaubern, retten, vergiften, töten.* In regard to the figures, ask questions such as:

Wie sehen sie aus? Was können sie? Was müssen sie tun?

You will also need a problem or a conflict that can be solved only by means of a task, an adventure, or a heroic deed. Remember, too, elements like the magic number 3; usually two attempts fail and the third is successful. In regard to the plot, ask questions such as:

Was passiert mit dem Helden? mit dem Bösewicht?

You may introduce an oral group-composition activity along these lines:

Wir schreiben jetzt ein Märchen. Wir brauchen also einen Helden oder eine Heldin, einen Bösewicht und einen Retter oder eine Retterin. Wer sind diese Personen? Wie sehen sie aus? Was können sie? Was müssen sie tun?

Then:

Deutsche Märchen beginnen mit „Es war einmal ....". Schreiben wir die ersten Sätze dieses Märchens.

Write a few simple sentences on the board to give students an idea of what you expect. Then have the students develop the fairy tale in small groups with key words in outline form. They should write the actual fairy tale for homework.

Cultural Note

Just like American real estate and apartment-wanted advertisements, German ads, listed under **Wohnungsmarkt** or **Immobilienmarkt**, rely heavily on abbreviations. Most of them are self-explanatory. **Miete 350 DM warm,** for example, means that (central) heat is included; **WW** refers to warm/hot water; a **3er WG** is a **Wohngemeinschaft** of three (unrelated) persons sharing an apartment. An apartment listed as **2 Zimmer, Küche, Bad, Balkon** (see realia, p. 93) may also be called a **Zweizimmerwohnung,** which does not refer to a two-bedroom apartment, but rather to an apartment with one bedroom and a living room. The **Bad** or **Badezimmer** is often listed since urban areas still have apartments without bathrooms or with only a shower installed next to the toilet.

Thema II: Jahreszeiten

Opening Photo

Have students come up with ten to twenty free associations based on the photo (p. 107).

Kapitel 4: Familienglück

EINSTIMMUNG: DAS FAMILIENLEBEN

To review vocabulary and to set the mood, ask questions about students' families. Sample questions:

> **Erinnern Sie sich noch?**
> **Wie war es, als Sie 15 waren?**
> **Wo haben Sie gewohnt?**
> **In welche Klasse sind Sie gegangen?**

Have students interview a partner using the questions in the text. Afterward, several students should report in plenum.

LESETEXT: VÄTER UND TÖCHTER

Vor dem Lesen

In preparation for the reading and the first activity, introduce the following vocabulary:

> **Flaum** = besonders leichte und weiche Feder
> **schweben** = die typische Bewegung von sehr leichten Dingen
> **verwundert** = erstaunt
> **Schein** = ungefähr: Licht
> **Augenbrauen** = Haare über den Augen
> **Krähenflügel** = die Flügel von Krähen
> **Krähe** = großer, schwarzer Vogel
> **schwingen** = hin und her, auf und ab bewegen
> **Gans** = großer, weißer Vogel mit langem Hals; in Deutschland ißt man Gans zu Weihnachten
> **Reißzwecke** = kleiner Nagel mit breitem, flachem Kopf

A. Wie man visuelle Informationen benutzt

Introduce the topic with the drawing (p. 110) and the questions provided. This is particularly effective if the drawing is reproduced and enlarged for overhead projection and the discussion takes place with books closed.

B. Vorhersagen machen

After students have read the English reading strategy, have them give answers to the questions. They should be encouraged to make guesses based on their own experience and their imagination. Afterward, let them read the text silently to determine how accurate their predictions were.

Nach dem Lesen

A. Ironischer Stil

For this relatively difficult activity you may need to provide support. Students should work in groups of three. Circulate among the groups to help out.

B. Schreiben Sie eine Zusammenfassung

For homework, have students reread the story. In the following class session, students should work in groups of three and write down the main elements of the story in short phrases. Have them practice retelling the story with the help of their notes. They should be discouraged from reading their notes aloud word for word.

Aktivitäten

A. Zeichnungen

This activity can be introduced by showing the drawing (p. 113) on the overhead (master provided in the **VMA**). Explain that the artistic quality of the drawing is not important; rather students should use the drawing to express feelings. Encourage students to respect the attempts of other students to express their feelings.

SPRECHAKTE: *BEGRÜSSEN/SICH VERABSCHIEDEN*

Do brainstorming as an introduction. Sample questions:

> **Wie begrüßen sich die Leute?**
> **Was ist anders in Deutschland als in den USA?**
> **Was sagen die Leute nicht?**

Write responses on the board. Then have students listen to the minidialogues. Sample questions:

> Dialogue 1: **Wo ruft die Studentin an? Warum? Was passiert?**
> Dialogue 2: **Warum ist Bärbel so in Eile? Was machen die beiden am Mittag?**

Role-play the situations without books.

Variationen

Spielen Sie!

Prepare in small groups, then role-play in plenum.

Photo and Realia

Have students learn about telephoning in the German-speaking countries with the help of the photo (p. 114) and the realia (p. 115). Compare the long distance costs with those in the United States. Ask, for example, why German rates are higher. Encourage students to speculate.

Cultural Note

The monopolies of the German **Bundespost** and the Austrian and Swiss postal services are much more inclusive than those of the U.S. Postal Service. Although the **Bundespost** has nominally split off some of its branches (in particular telecommunications, where there is now some competition), it still controls mail, telephone, teletype, and telefax communication, provides all facilities for radio and television transmission, and installs and maintains the relatively new cable TV network, to name only a few functions. This may account for delays in the introduction of high-tech services such as the mobile telephone network and the high cost of renting or purchasing items such as portable phones for the home. It may also account for the high telephone charges even after the greatly touted latest rate reduction (see realia, p. 115): a three-minute call from Germany to the United States costs up to four times as much as from the United States to Germany. Nonetheless, basic services such as mail and parcel post delivery are of unsurpassed reliability and speed; overnight first-class delivery (without any surcharge) is virtually assured between larger cities.

LESETEXT: PAPA, CHARLY HAT GESAGT . . .

Vor dem Lesen

Vorbereitung auf den Text

Discuss the questions in plenum.

Cultural Note

Young people reach legal maturity in Germany at age 18, in Austria at 19, and in Switzerland at 20. In Germany, at 18 one may also acquire a driver's license, get married without consent, and consume liquor in public without being accompanied by a parent or a guardian. Consumption of beer or wine is, however, permitted at age 16.

Nach dem Lesen

B. Was steht im Text?

Since this text is relatively long, you may wish to divide it into several small segments to use with this activity. Suggested breakdown (question numbers refer to **Nach dem Lesen,** exercise B):

> **Zeile 1–36 mit Fragen 1–6**
> **Zeile 37–102 mit Fragen 7–9**
> **Zeile 103–143 und Fragen 10–12**

Students may read the sections and answer the questions in groups. Discuss the questions briefly in plenum.
    As an alternative and to check global comprehension, have the groups invent (sub)titles for the various sections of the story. You may wish to do the first section as a demonstration for the entire class, then have students work in groups of three. Suggested breakdown:

> **Zeile 1–30; Zeile 31–51; Zeile 52–61; Zeile 62–74; Zeile 75–97; Zeile 98–107; Zeile 108–124; Zeile 125–136; Zeile 137–143**

As a wrap-up, write the titles on the board and discuss.

Aktivitäten

A. Was meinen Sie?

As an introduction or follow-up, ask questions such as:

> Wer kennt jemanden, der mit einem Freund oder mit einer Freundin zusammenlebt?
> Wer hat ein Familienmitglied, das sowas macht?
> Wer von Ihnen lebt mit dem Freund oder der Freundin zusammen?

Read through the possibilities with the students, then have them work in small groups to try to reach a consensus. Have groups report in plenum and discuss.

SPRECHAKTE: *SICH/JEMANDEN VORSTELLEN*

Read the minidialogues and ask questions such as:

> Dialogue 1: **Woher kennt Uwe Andreas? Wohin gehen sie?**
> Dialogue 2: **Weswegen kommt Rita? Wie stellt man sich vor? Wie stellt man andere vor?**

Write elicited expressions on the board.

Variationen

Spielen Sie!

Divide the class into pairs. Each pair should practice one of the three situations and then perform the scene for the class.

UND JETZT ZU IHNEN!

As a preparation for the first role play, work with the class to come up with reasons why one's son or daughter should not move out of the house. Students should practice the role plays in pairs or small groups. Afterward, have some groups present their dialogues to the class.

Kapitel 5: Generationen

Opening Photo

Brainstorm with students to elicit associations with the photo (p. 138) and to draw attention to the irony of an older man in a child's swing. Talk about the concept of a "second childhood" and how such a term might arise. Move directly to the **Einstimmung** photo.

EINSTIMMUNG: ALTE MENSCHEN IN DER GESELLSCHAFT

Photo

With the photo (p. 139), continue brainstorming about the activities of older people. What are these people doing? Where are they going? Why? Why together? Draw an associogram for *alt* or *alt werden* on the board. Sample questiosn:

> **Wann ist man alt?**
> **Wie wird man alt?**
> **Was verbinden Sie mit „alt werden"?**

B. Was assoziieren Sie mit alten Menschen?

Ask students about the connotations of the words in the box. Sample question:

Welche dieser Ausdrücke sind eher positiv, welche eher negativ?

Have students come up with five other concepts related to the topic of old age.

LESETEXT: EIN MORGEN IN DER STADT
Cultural Note

On the first day of elementary school, parents give their children a cone-shaped **Schultüte** (literally, *school bag*) (see photo, p. 140) filled with all sorts of candy and fruit to "sweeten" the traumatic experience of having to go to school.

Vor dem Lesen
Vorhersagen machen

With books closed, use the board for a brainstorming session. Possible approach:

Eine alte Frau und eine junge Frau treffen sich auf der Straße. Sie sehen sich kurz an und gehen weiter. Was denkt die junge Frau? Was denkt die alte Frau?

Make two lists on the board.

Nach dem Lesen

As a follow-up, have students work in groups after they have read the text. Sample questions for group discussion:

Was findet die junge Frau am Alter gut?
Was findet die alte Frau an der Jugend gut?

Afterward discuss in plenum the students' answers and compare their ideas with the content in the text. After students have done exercises A and B, have them reread the text once or twice before they do C.

LESETEXT: ALT WERDEN
Vor dem Lesen

With books closed, do an associogram for **alt werden** on the board or with an overhead projector.

Aktivitäten

A. Wer, was, wann, wo und warum?

Have students describe the drawings before completing the sentences. Sample questions:

Wie alt ist diese Person?
Was macht er/sie?
Ist das typisch?

Kapitel 5

SPRECHAKTE: *MITGEFÜHL AUSDRÜCKEN*

Variationen

Use the obituary notices (p. 146) to elicit vocabulary. Discuss the German practice of friends and co-workers placing such notices in newspapers when someone dies instead of sending flowers. Work through the information in the notices. Sample questions:

> **Wie hieß diese Person?**
> **Wann wurde sie geboren?** (As an aside, you may wish to explain hat **geboren werden** is used for those who have died, whereas *geboren sein* is used for the living.)
> **Wie alt wurde sie?**
> **Wann findet die Beerdigung statt? Wo?**

Cultural Note

German, Austrian, and Swiss newspapers do not carry obituary columns. Instead, the family of the deceased takes out a paid announcement (**Todesanzeige**) that gives information on the funeral arrangements, church service(s), and burial. It is usually signed by the immediate family members of the deceased.

Vor dem Lesen

Vorbereitung auf den Text

Introduce your students to German-German dictionaries (Wahrig, Duden, and others). Show students how to use them, and discuss their advantages and disadvantages.

Nach dem Lesen

A. Steht das im Text?

Help students correct the incorrect sentences.

Cultural Note

Asbach Uralt is the best-selling German **Weinbrand** (*brandy*). Though popularly known as **Kognak**, **Weinbrand** is the official designation for brandy. One of the many clauses of the 1919 Treaty of Versailles, which formally ended World War I, contained a provision prohibiting Germans from selling their brandy under the French term "cognac"; another curtailed the patent rights of German chemical companies in the United States, such as Bayer Leverkusen. This led to the mass production of inexpensive aspirin in the United States, while in Germany it is still produced only by Bayer Leverkusen and sold at a relatively high price.

C. Was meinen Sie?

You may want to help students supplement their vocabularies for this type of activity. Simply provide words orally and on the board as the need arises. These words may appear later in worksheets or on exams, but only in a passive context. Students should never be expected to have an active command of words that come up in such situations.

Aktivitäten

B. Wortassoziationen

Read these words to the students:

> **glücklich, alt, einsam, zufrieden, müde, deprimiert, froh, weise, verlassen, langweilig**

Kapitel 6: Reifeprüfung

Opening Photo

Using the photo (p. 166), establish a context for the chapter. Help students brainstorm about the photo. Sample questions:

> **Wer sind diese jungen Leute?**
> **Was machen sie?**
> **Wo sind sie?**
> **Warum?**

EINSTIMMUNG: PROBLEME DEUTSCHER JUGENDLICHER

Interaktion

As a follow-up activity, exploit the three pieces of realia (p. 167) to develop vocabulary and to explore the chapter context more deeply. Sample questions:

> **„Zum Berufswechsel bereit": Was ist das Thema?**

If you do not get a (correct) response, write **Berufswechsel** on the board, split the word into its two parts, and lead the students to an understanding of the word: **Beruf** < **ruf(en)**, vgl. engl. *to call* and *calling*—that is, *vocation*; **Wechsel**, vgl. **Wechselstube, Geldwechsel**.

> **Welche Berufe erkennen Sie?**

Help students recognize names or parts of names of occupations—for example, **-handel-, -kauf-, Verkäufer, Bank-, Büro-, Bäcker, Mechaniker, Arzt-, -helfer-, Friseurin, Köche**, and so on.

> **„ZUM BERUFSWECHSEL BEREIT"**
> **Wozu sind die Fachkräfte bereit?**
> **Von hundert Bäckern, wie viele sind bereit, einen anderen Beruf auszuüben?**
>
> **„WEISSAGUNG DER CREE"**
> **Welche Wörter erkennen Sie?**
> **Was ist mit dem Baum? dem Fluß? dem Fisch? dem Geld?**
> **„Weissagung" bedeutet Sprichwort. Kennen Sie ein anderes deutsches (amerikanisches) Sprichwort?**
>
> **„WALDSTERBEN"**
> **Was ist das Thema?**
> **Wieviel von dem Wald ist schon geschädigt?**
> **Wie war früher der Wald?**
> **Wer hat diese Werbung geschrieben/bezahlt?**
> **Wer sollte dieses Formular ausfüllen?**
> **Würden Sie dieses Formular ausfüllen?**

LESETEXT: SACKGASSE FÜR DIE JUGEND?

Vor dem Lesen

As an introduction to the reading, do an associogram on the board: **Probleme der Jugendliche**.

Cultural Note

Radio and television stations are privately owned and operated in the United States (although licensed and supervised by FCC); however, in Germany, Austria, and Switzerland stations are semipublic or semi-government operations. In Germany, for example, they legally function as **Anstalt(en) des Öffentlichen Rechts** (*institutions under public jurisdiction*). This means that public figures and government-selected politicians serve on the **Beirat** (*administrative council*) that establishes the policy and direction each station will take.

Each of the states has its own radio network or cooperates with a neighboring state (**Bayerischer Rundfunk, Hessischer Rundfunk, Südwestfunk Baden-Baden, Radio Bremen**). There may be several "contrast" programs operated by one station. All are coordinated by the **Arbeitsgemeinschaft der Öffentlich- Rechtlichen Rundfunkanstalten der Bundesrepublik Deutschland, ARD** for short. After World War II, Germany's AM broadcast frequencies were severely curtailed. Because its range of transmission is more limited and does not interfere as much with stations in surrounding countries, FM was developed in Germany earlier than in the United States. Today, most of the broadcasting is in FM stereo.

The operation of the first postwar television stations in West Germany was a costly undertaking. The federal government coordinated its efforts under the umbrella of the **ARD** in what is now called the **Erstes Programm,** to which all states contribute program segments. Thus, nationwide television programming began in the early 50s. Several years later another network, **Zweites Deutsches Fernsehen,** was founded in Mainz. It does not rely on the states for program feeds but instead produces original segments. Most of the states have a **Drittes Programm,** which, like PBS in the United States, features issues of regional interest as well as high-quality programs of general interest.

Funding for the three networks originally came exclusively from the **Hörfunk- und Fernsehgebühren** that each radio and TV subscriber must pay. Currently, the fee is about DM 50,- for both radio and television every three months. **Schwarzhören** and **Schwarzsehen** (that is, unauthorized radio or TV use) are subject to stiff penalties, and the **Bundespost**, which operates the technical installations nationwide, has special locator vans (**Peilwagen**) that can spot TV sets in operation and check whether the user is on the subscriber list. In the last two decades, TV commercials have increasingly augmented funding. However, contrary to the U.S. custom, all commercials are shown together during the late afternoon and early evening hours and do not interrupt major programming.

Since the introduction of cable television in the early 1980s, there has been a proliferation of new, commercial TV stations, many of them relying on satellite transmission (SAT 1, 3 SAT). Cable TV subscribers, who must pay a surcharge for cable TV service in addition to the regular radio and TV fees, can now receive programs from neighboring countries in several languages—for example, TV 5 from France and Super Channel from Britain. Some of the new stations have also introduced 24-hour operations, totally unknown in Germany until recently.

A. *Fremdwörter*

Read the words aloud and have the students repeat them. Cognates with English are often mispronounced, since students may have the tendency to pronounce them as if they were English. After reading the list, ask about the text. Write responses on the board. Sample questions:

> **Wovon, glauben Sie, handelt der folgende Text?**
> **Dieser Text ist ein Teil einer Fernsehdiskussion zum Thema „Probleme der Jugendlichen."**
> **Es diskutieren Jugendliche mit einem Psychiater, einem Journalisten und einem Politiker. Welche Themen werden wohl diskutiert?**

Nach dem Lesen

G. *Diskutieren Sie mit*

Do as a group activity. Then have each group share its results with the entire class. Let each group, in turn, take over the role of the instructor, such that students sit before the class and the instructor retires to the rear of the room. Other students take notes and ask questions.

Aktivitäten

A. *Interaktion*

As an introduction, ask students to identify the situations depicted in drawings (p. 173) and determine what is embarrassing about them. Sample questions:

> Wo ist das?
> Was macht diese Person? *or:* Was machen diese Personen?
> Warum ist das peinlich? *or:* Ist das peinlich?
> Wäre Ihnen das auch peinlich?

Clarification of situations:

> Man is smoking in an elevator under a "No Smoking" sign.
> Two women discover that they are wearing the same dress at a party.
> A man at the theater box office can't seem to find his money.
> Two people talking loudly during a movie.
> A man "steals" a taxi from a woman during a rain storm.
> A man misses his train.
> A woman sitting on a park bench doesn't see the "fresh paint" sign.
> A student gets several poor grades on his report card.

Model a possible response for a couple of the situations. Possible responses:

> Ich hätte den Mann gebeten, nicht zu rauchen.
> Ich hätte diesen Leuten gesagt, sie sollten schweigen.
> Ich wäre nach Hause gegangen und hätte ein neues Kleid angezogen.

Then have each student find a partner to discuss the remaining situations. Encourage students to repeat what you have said in plenum about each situation so that they practice describing the situation as well as explaining what they would have done.

B. *Was meinen Sie?*

Prepare the students for this activity by asking whether they are for or against nuclear power plants (**Atomkraftwerke**). Expand on the structure using a **da**-compound with a **daß**-clause. Sample questions:

> Ich bin gegen Atomkraftwerke. Sind Sie auch dagegen, oder sind Sie dafür?
> Ich bin dagegen, daß man neue Atomkraftwerke baut. Sind Sie auch dagegen, daß man neue Atomkraftwerke baut?

Write the two structures on the board:

> Ich bin gegen _____.
>
> Ich bin dagegen, daß _____.

Then expand on the activity. Sample questions:

> **Wer von Ihnen ist gegen Atomwaffen? Warum?**

Write several reasons on the board; begin each reason with **weil**. Point out the subordinate word order to students. Have students silently mark five things that they are against and write one reason for each. Their reasons should begin with **weil**. If they cannot find five things they are against, have them add additional things to the list.

Kapitel 6

C. Umfrage

As an alternative, do a recombination exercise:

> **Stehen Sie auf, gehen Sie im Klassenzimmer herum und fragen Sie fünf verschiedene Leute, wogegen sie sind. Fragen Sie auch „warum", und machen Sie sich Notizen.**

Ask students whom they spoke with, what that person was against, and what the reason was. Pick a few sample reasons and write them correctly as models on the board with **weil**.

D. Fernsehinterview

Provide a model and develop vocabulary by letting a proficient student with a loud voice ask you the questions. Other students should have their books closed. You should answer briefly, in simple sentences, but with a varied vocabulary and sentence structure. Have students note the vocabulary you use. Say, for example:

> **Welche Redemittel benutze ich?**
> **Schreiben Sie auf, was Sie hören.**

Possible answers:

> **Ich finde sie eigentlich ganz gut.**
> **Ich bin eigentlich dagegen, weil sie so gefährlich sind.**
> **Unsere Steuern sind zu niedrig. Meiner Meinung nach müssen sie erhöht werden.**

As the students read the vocabulary they have collected, write it on the board. Students should then interview a partner. Afterward, have two or three pairs do their interviews in plenum. Repeat with the film star interview in a subsequent class session.

Cultural Note

While the united Germany will continue the draft, military duty has been cut from 18 to 12 months. In addition, troops will be substantially reduced. The former East German army (**Nationale Volksarmee**) will be under West German command and will serve as a territorial force; its troops will not be part of Germany's NATO contingent. The Russian troops currently stationed on former East German territory will be withdrawn by 1994.

LESETEXT: JUGEND IN DER DDR

Cultural Note

Die Bundeszentrale für politische Bildung in Bonn ist eine Institution, die von keiner Partei abhängig ist.

Cultural Note

Dieser Text wurde noch 1989 in einer Neuauflage veröffenlicht, also im selben Jahr, als die Öffnung der Mauer die Ereignisse in Gang setzte, die letzlich zur deutschen Einheit im Oktober 1990 geführt haben. Dieser Text ist somit nicht nur ein historisches Dokument, sondern gibt auch Einblicke in psychologische und soziale Unterschiede zwischen Menschen aus Ost und West. Politisch und auf dem Papier sind die Deutschen inzwischen ein geeintes Volk, aber der Prozeß des Zusammenwachsens kann eben nur allmählich erfolgen.

Vor dem Lesen

Prepare students for the reading with a general discussion. Sample questions:

> Was meinen Sie, gibt es größere Unterschiede zwischen Deutschen aus dem Norden und Süden oder aus dem Osten und Westen der Bundesrepublik? Warum?
> Geben Sie Beispiele für Unterschiede (Sprache, Kultur, Religion, Politik, Geschichte usw.)

Cultural Note

This text contains historically relevant references to the privileged class of the former GDR, which included many members of the former SED (**Sozialistische Einheitspartei Deutschlands**, or *Socialist Unity Party*). Since the events of November 1989, all (West) German parties have established themselves in the eastern part of the country. Early in 1990, the leaders of the SED decided to change their name to PDS (**Partei des Demokratischen Sozialismus**) in order to play down the now damaging reference to East German socialism that had obviously been a euphemistic term for communism. The name change did not stop the huge number of party defections; people returned their membership cards by the thousands. In the first free all-German election after Hitler's rise to power, December 2, 1990, the PDS received only 0.3% of the vote in the western states of Germany; it is highly unlikely that the PDS will play any significant role in the future.

Nach dem Lesen

Photo

Do an associogram for the photo (p. 179). Sample questions:

> Welche Assoziationen haben Sie beim Anblick dieses Photos?
> Fallen Ihnen ähnliche Bilder aus der Geschichte oder aus anderen Teilen der Welt ein?

B. Sprache und Politik

Introduce the activity by asking:

> Welche Begriffe oder Schlagwörter gibt es in der Politik der USA, die nur im politischen Zusammenhang zu verstehen sind?

C. *Vergleichen Sie!*

This activity is designed to summarize the two readings. However, since the readings deal with historical situations, the question arises, which problems are currently being dealt with. Ask:

> Wie haben sich die Probleme inzwischen verändert, angeglichen, oder gibt es vielleicht ganz neue?

Aktivitäten

A. Was ist passiert?

Do first as a group activity, then repeat in a subsequent class session as an individual activity.

B. Vorurteile

Give students a few minutes to complete the activity or assign it the day before as homework. Then go over selected items in the list where problems might have occurred. Discuss the difference between the real situation and the cliché. For which clichés is there a kernel of truth? For which not?

C. Stereotype

Have students provide possible conclusions to the sentences and write them on the board. Note: all require *zu + adjective*. Develop some patterns with students, using their suggestions and other words you provide.

E. Gruppenarbeit

In the interest of time, have one group find clichés and another group prejudices. Then have each group report in plenum.

LESETEXT: LYRIK

Before the reading, briefly explain what a **Reifezeugnis** is and compare it to the American diploma. With books closed, read the poem to the class with the aid of an overhead projector. As you read, cover or uncover what the speaker **bekam**. Then do a group activity in which students complete the text on the overhead. Remind students that the verb *bekommen* requires an accusative object and that it is a false cognate. Tell them the old German joke:

> **Ein Deutscher kommt eines Tages in ein amerikanisches Restaurant und bestellt ein Steak. Da er das deutsche Wort** *bekommen* **kennt, sagt er: „I become a steak."**

Finally, have students open their books and compare the text with their work on the transparency.

Thema III: Zwischen zwei Welten

Opening Photo

Use the photo of foreign youths in Lindau at Lake Constance (p. 197) to help students get into the unit theme. Sample questions:

> **Wo ist das?**
> **Wer sind diese Kinder?** (türkische Kinder)
> **Wo sind sie?** (auf dem Spielplatz)
> **Was machen Türken in Deutschland?**
> **Wie fühlen sie sich?**
> **Wie würden Sie sich fühlen, wenn Sie Ausländer wären?**
> **Warum leben diese Menschen „zwischen zwei Welten"?**

Kapitel 7: Heimat in der Fremde

Opening Photo

Exploit the photo (p. 198) in a similar fashion as the **Thema III** photo (p. 197).

EINSTIMMUNG: HEIMAT IN DER FREMDE

Guide students with questions and comments to generate the two lists on the board, in two columns.

Cultural Note

The notion of **Gastarbeiter** is nothing new in recent German history. Even before the turn of the century, Polish workers came to northern Germany to harvest the huge potato crops; many of them remained in Germany at that time. During World War II, great numbers of **Fremdarbeiter** were forcibly moved to

Großdeutschland to work in ammunition plants and on farms or to repair war damage. In 1945, they formed a large part of the so-called "Displaced Persons," or DPs, who needed to be repatriated or resettled.

West Germany reached full employment in 1957–1958. After the borders were sealed with the building of the Berlin Wall in 1961, it could no longer draw on East German workers to increase its labor force. Therefore, foreign workers were invited (hence the new term **Gastarbeiter**) to come to West Germany. Initial recruitment occurred primarily in Austria and in certain Mediterranean countries such as Italy and Greece. When active recruitment was stopped in 1973, there were some 2.6 million workers from these areas as well as from Yugoslavia, Turkey, and Spain. In addition, the German economic miracle (**Wirtschaftswunder**) attracted workers and their families from as far as Portugal, Algeria, Morocco, and Tunisia. Although the number of workers dropped to about 1.6 million in 1986, there are still nearly 4.5 million foreigners living in Germany. Guest workers now constitute the largest minority in (West) Germany. Before the onset of a new immigration wave of Germans from countries like Poland and Russia in the late 1980s and the opening of the Berlin Wall, guest workers accounted for 65% of the relative population increase in West Germany.

In this last decade of the century, almost 60% of the foreigners will have stayed in (West) Germany for more than 10 years; more than two thirds of the foreign children have been born in Germany. In some metropolitan areas, 20% of the population are foreign nationals; the 1.4 million Turks are particularly concentrated in large urban areas, where their different ethnic, cultural and religious background makes it especially difficult for them to assimilate. This has led to friction at all levels of society: Turkish children experience problems in school and on the playgrounds, while their working parents encounter hidden or overt discrimination at the workplace.

Increasing unemployment in (West) Germany, (between 8% and 9% before the opening of the East-West German border in November 1989) hit especially the more than half a million Turkish guest workers hard. Having long since considered themselves "second-class citizens," whether they had acquired German citizenship or not, many feel relegated to a third rank, now that so many East Germans are trying to find employment in the West.

With the ever-increasing population of second-generation children of guest workers reaching adult age, a sizable body of literature on the plight of the guest workers has been produced by socially engaged German authors, by writers from these foreign countries, and also by German-born second-generation members of this group. Many of these writings deal with the special problems women and children of guest workers have to face in contemporary German society.

While Switzerland has historically had a great influx of primarily Italian guest workers, labor laws and immigration regulations have always been tougher than those in postwar (West) Germany. Seasonal workers (**Saisonniers**) are allowed to spend only nine months a year in Switzerland and may not bring their families with them.

The recent opening of East Germany has brought to light the little-known fact that the former GDR had invited guest workers, too. There was a well-publicized "friendship" campaign in the 1960s to extend a helping hand to Cubans disadvantaged after the cut-off of relations with the United States, but it was little known that the GDR recruited North Korean and Vietnamese workers to fill the void left by its shrinking population. The workers came without their families, were on five-year contracts with one free trip home in between; they were housed in separate compounds that allowed hardly any contact with the German population. Most of them were "repatriated" when mass unemployment began to rear its head in East Germany in 1990, contract or not.

LESETEXT: DU BIST KEIN DEUTSCHER

Follow the **Einstimmung** with a brainstorming session. Compile lists on the board. (1) For what reasons did foreigners come to the Federal Republic? (2) What problems do they have, and what problems do they allegedly cause?

Realia: „Das Land, das die Fremden nicht beschützt, geht bald unter."

Possible questions about the illustration on p. 200.

Was sagt Ihnen diese Broschüre über die Situation von Ausländern in der Bundesrepublik?
Was glauben Sie, gibt es Ausländer, die eher willkommen sind als andere?
Aus welchen Ländern kommen sie (nicht)?
Die vier Verbände, die diese Broschüre herausgeben, sind karikativer oder sozialer Natur.

Vor dem Lesen

Teach students about children's games (**Kinderspiele**). For example, ask:

Was spielen Kinder?

Make a list of German and American children's games on the board. Describe a game to students in German. Have individual students explain another game to the class.

Deutsche Kinderspiele: Fangen, Verstecken, Ballspiele

You may wish to introduce a German counting rhyme (**Abzählreim**) such as:

Ich und du,
Müllers Kuh,
Müllers Esel der bist du;
Enemenemaus
und du bist raus.

Compare English rhymes such as "One potato, two potato, . . . "

B. *Notizen zur Handlung*

Collect these notes orally, writing them on the board or on a transparency. Have students work in small groups to formulate summaries of the plot, then retell the story in plenum.

Nach dem Lesen

Have students reread the first three paragraphs silently. Then ask:

Was möchte Ender spielen?
Warum spielt Stefan nicht mit ihm?
Wie reagiert Ender darauf?
Wie sieht Ender aus?
Woher, glauben Sie, kommt er?
Was ist der wahre Grund dafür, daß Stefan nicht mit Ender spielen möchte?

Have students reread the story in its entirety at home. As an alternative, check global comprehension:

Sind diese Aussagen richtig (r) oder falsch (f)? Machen Sie aus falschen Aussagen richtige.

1. Der kleine Türke heißt Stefan.
2. Stefan will nicht mit Ender spielen, weil Ender kein Deutscher ist.
3. Ender ist das egal.
4. Zwei deutsche Kinder sammeln im Park Kastanien.
5. Die deutschen Kinder sind unfreundlich zu Ender. Sie wollen ihm angst machen.
6. Ender sagt: „Die Kastanien gehören allen. Jeder kann im Park Kastanien sammeln."
7. Ender kämpft mit den beiden deutschen Kindern.
8. Zu Hause fragt Ender seine Mutter, ob er Türke oder Deutscher sei.
9. Seine Mutter sagt ihm, daß er Ender sei.

10. Enders Eltern sind in Deutschland aufgewachsen und zur Schule gegangen. Sie können gut Deutsch.
11. Ender spricht besser Türkisch als Deutsch.
12. Ender geht in die erste Klasse einer deutschen Schule. Er spricht Deutsch wie seine Muttersprache.
13. Der Unterschied zwischen ihm und den anderen Kindern ist, daß sie kein Türkisch können.
14. Als Ender seinen Vater fragt, ob er Deutscher oder Türke sei, weiß der Vater nicht, was er sagen soll.
15. Der Vater will mit Stefan sprechen, damit er wieder mit Ender spielt.

Aktivitäten

A. *Was würden Sie tun?*

Give students a few minutes to formulate answers to the questions or assign the preparation as homework.
   For a recombination activity, have each student find a partner to go along on a dream vacation. Students should go around the room and ask three other students:

Wie stellst du dir deine Traumreise vor?

Then ask other questions in the list, as appropriate. Finally, each student should choose one of the three people he/she interviewed to go on the trip and report to the class. The class should then decide whether the "right" partner was chosen for the trip. As an alternative for homework, have students write a letter to a friend about a dream vacation they have taken.

B. *Interaktion*

Use the drawing of the travel poster (p. 207) to elicit vocabulary:

die Schweiz, der Berg, der Schnee, die Kirche, der Fluß, das (Segel)Boot, die Kuh, die Wolke, der Himmel usw.

Review "positional" vocabulary (**oben, unten, links, rechts, in der Mitte**). Then have students work in pairs to describe the poster. Afterwards, have a few students provide descriptions in plenum as a check of vocabulary and structure.

Cultural Note

Nearly half of all vacationing (West) Germans tour their own country. Germans, on the whole, are among the most avid world travelers. With 94% of the work force entitled to at least five weeks of vacation and with one of the highest incomes per capita, (West) Germans can indeed afford to take two or three vacations a year. The advantageous exchange rate of the dollar has made the United States a favorite vacation place; Germans rent cars or campers and often travel across the entire continent. Even students can cross the Atlantic on low-cost flights such as the ones advertised (p. 205). The true bargain prices frequently require charter travel or flights on less desirable carriers; 24-hour delays in less-than-comfortable airports are not uncommon. Still, in 1989 a flight around the world for DM 2399,- was indeed a bargain.

SPRECHAKTE: *UM ERLAUBNIS BITTEN*

Use the dialogue as a listening comprehension activity. Before, reading the dialogue, ask questions such as:

Dialogue 1: **Was möchte Elisabeth? Warum darf sie das nicht? wann? mit wem? womit? Wie alt ist sie?**
Dialogue 2: **Was hätte Klaus machen sollen? Bis wann möchte er es machen? Geht das? Was war das Thema des Aufsatzes? Wohin sollen die Studenten ihre Aufsätze legen?**

Make three columns on the board: **um Erlaubnis bitten / erlauben / Erlaubnis verweigern.** Have students suggest expressions, taken from dialogues or elsewhere, for each column.

Variationen

B. Spielen Sie!

In preparation for this activity, have students work in small groups and suggest two or three expressions or sentences for each situation. Afterward, write the best choices on the board. Then have students prepare and rehearse the situations with a partner. Afterward, one or two pairs should perform the situation in plenum.

Cultural Note

The German monthly *Geo*, inspired by *National Geographic*, is a beautifully illustrated journal devoted to geographic, anthropological, sociocultural, and environmental topics. In addition to the regular issues, *Geo* publishes *Geo-Special*, special editions that feature a particular country such as Switzerland or, more recently—and just before the unification of Germany—the GDR.

LESETEXT: MUSTERDEMOKRATIE SCHWEIZ

Vor dem Lesen

A. Komposita

Have students practice using German-German dictionaries. In small groups, they should look up and discuss the meanings of the compound words by naming synonyms or related words. As an alternative ask:

> Welche Bedeutung haben diese Wörter im Kontext?
> 1. Der Schlüssel zur Musterdemokratie liegt in dem Recht zur *Volksabstimmung*.
>   a. Frauen dürfen wählen
>   b. das Volk ist ein Modell
>   c. das Volk entscheidet
> 2. In keiner anderen Demokratie können die Bürger so unmittelbar bei der *Gesetzgebung* mitbestimmen wie in der Schweiz.
>   a. Legislative
>   b. Wahl von Politikern
>   c. Verurteilung von Kriminellen
> 3. Zum dritten Mal wollte eine politisch rechte Gruppe die *Überfremdung* der Schweiz beenden. Von den 1,06 Millionen Ausländern sollten 500 000 das Land verlassen.
>   a. Import und Export von Waren
>   b. Geld aus dem Ausland ist im Land
>   c. zu viele Ausländer sind im Land
> 4. Beim fakultativen Referendum wird über jedes Bundesgesetz vom Volk entschieden, wenn 50 000 Schweizer oder acht *Kantone* es wollen.
>   a. Bundesland der Schweiz
>   b. Stadt in China
>   c. politische Partei
> 5. Daß die *Saisonarbeiter* mehr Rechte bekommen sollten, gefiel den Hotelbesitzern nicht.
>   a. Hotelgäste, die nur im Frühling und im Sommer da sind
>   b. Arbeiter, die nur in einer bestimmten Jahreszeit arbeiten
>   c. Italiener und Franzosen

Cultural Note

The spoken local language of German-speaking Switzerland is **Schweizerdeutsch** or, as it is often transcribed, **Schwyzerdytsch, Schwyzerdütsch,** or **Schwyzertütsch**. It belongs to the high Alemannic family of German and, as the two samples of the Lord's Prayer indicate (pp. 207, 209), differs dramatically from standard High German. In fact, the average German will not be able to understand much

Schwyzerdütsch, although reading it may be slightly easier. The sample texts and the phonetic spelling variants of the name of the language show that there are "cantonal" or regional variants, such as **Züritüütsch** around Zürich and **Bärndütsch** in the area of the capital, Bern.

Swiss children learn standard High German in school. Since this is an acquired, almost second language for many, their command of High German is generally very good. In the German-speaking area of the country, Swiss radio and television carry some programs in **Schwyzerdütsch;** the main Swiss radio station in German-speaking Switzerland, Radio Beromünster, also features a shortwave service in high Alemannic for Swiss emigrants worldwide.

Aktivitäten

A. Wo möchten Sie hin?

Take a poll, writing popular and unpopular countries on the board and listing reasons for and against travel to each.

Kapitel 8: Auf der Suche nach America

Opening Photo

Use the photo (p. 224) to guide students in a brainstorming session about Mickey Mouse. Do an associogram with Mickey Mouse in the center to elicit responses like cartoon, Disney, Mickey Mouse Club, Disneyland, and others.

EINSTIMMUNG: ASSOZIATIONEN

Do two associograms, one on the left side of the board, one on the right. On the left:

Was assoziieren Sie mit den USA?

On the right:

Was, glauben Sie, assoziiert man in Deutschland mit den USA?

Realia

Use the TV schedule (p. 225) to review telling time and prepositions of time as well as for cultural insights. Sample questions:

In welchem Programm sieht man diese Sendungen?
Was kommt um 21.45?
Wie heißt diese Episode?
Wer spielt mit?
Was passiert in dieser Episode?
Welche anderen amerikanischen Sendungen kommen heute?

Realia

Using the chart of German immigration figures (p. 225), ask questions to have students retrieve information from the chart. Practice reading large numbers aloud.

Cultural Note

The statistics on German immigration to the United States from 1820 to 1970 show that the absolute percentage peak of total immigration was reached after the 1848 revolution, which resulted in a conservative backlash and much disillusionment among younger Germans. In addition, news of the gold rush in California contributed to the wave of immigration. In this century, there were two waves of German emigrants to the United States. Both occurred in the decades following the two world wars—the second wave not beginning until the 1950s, since Germans were not freely admitted immediately after 1945.

LESETEXT: EINE UMFRAGE IN DER BRD

Cultural Note

The **Friedrich-Ebert-Stiftung** is one of the oldest political foundations in Germany, established in 1925 in memory of Friedrich Ebert (1871–1925) who, from 1919–1925, was the first **Reichspräsident** of the Weimar Republic. A member of the SPD, he was one of the most important statesmen this party produced between the two world wars. The Foundation, forbidden in 1933 and reestablished in 1947, is active in a number of areas such as providing scholarships for young students and returning adult students and establishing training programs in underdeveloped countries.

The two other major German parties also support political foundations: In 1964, one year after the resignation of Konrad Adenauer (1876–1967) as the first **Bundeskanzler** (*chancellor*) of the Federal Republic, the CDU established the **Konrad-Adenauer-Stiftung für politische Bildung und Studienförderung.** This foundation, as its title indicates, promotes political awareness and provides fellowship monies. Theodor Heuss (1884–1963), from 1949–1959 the first president of the Federal Republic and one of the leading liberal (FDP) politicians of the postwar era, founded the **Friedrich-Naumann-Stiftung** in 1958. Its goal is the dissemination of liberal ideas, especially among the adult population.

Vor dem Lesen: 1. Teil

Vorhersagen machen

With books closed, list some of the items on the board. Have students vote whether or not the Germans would consider the term positive or negative. Hold onto the results. Sample questions:

> **Wie sehen die Deutschen Ihrer Meinung nach die folgenden amerikanischen Importe: positiv, negativ oder neutral?**

Have students work in small groups with the entire list. They should compare their conclusions with the statistics in part 1 of the text and report back to the class. Do not let them look ahead.

Nach dem Lesen

A. *Interpretation der Tabelle*

Use free conversation in plenum to exploit the table (p. 227). Collect students' answers on the overhead or on the board and compare.

Cultural Note

As the extremely positive rating of John F. Kennedy in the opinion poll (p. 227) indicates, no other American politician since Abraham Lincoln has remained so high in the average German's awareness. Germans have not forgotten Kennedy's support of their country and of West Berlin, in particular, when it became isolated after the 1961 construction of the Wall. People still chuckle when they quote his famous, though unintentionally humorous, words uttered before more than 100,000 citizens in front of the Berlin-Schöneberg city hall: **Ich bin ein Berliner** (*ein* **Berliner** = *jelly doughnut*). With the exception of perhaps Walt Disney, no other 20th-century American seems to have had a greater impact on modern day Germans.

Aktivitäten

A. Wer ist das?

This should be done as a recombination activity. Sample instructions:

> **Stehen Sie auf, gehen Sie im Klassenzimmer herum und stellen Sie Ihren Mitstudenten Fragen, um die Aufgabe zu lösen.**
> **Schreiben Sie neben jede Frage den Namen eines Studenten/einer Studentin, auf dem/die diese Eigenschaft zutrifft.**

Follow up during the next class session by posing the ten questions in plenum.

B. Welche Fragen gefallen mir?

Read through the list with students to insure understanding. Students should prepare the activity as homework, by marking the questions they like with + and those they don't like with –. For the "+ questions," have students write down the name of another student to whom they would like to pose the questions. Finally, they should answer the questions themselves, in short sentences. On the following day, form small groups. For a period of about five minutes, one student in each group answers questions posed by the other students in the group. Afterward, the student who answered the questions may ask each of the other students one question which he/she has answered.

As an alternative, have the students in each group take turns answering the questions. Each student asks two questions before another student is chosen to answer the questions; or do this as a recombination activity, in which students move around the classroom asking questions of various students. Each of the alternatives should be closed with an "accountability" activity in plenum.

C. Wie mache ich das?

You may wish to demonstrate, or have a student demonstrate, these depicted positions (p. 230, top) in TPR (total physical response). If you are willing to demonstrate, your students will willingly and enthusiastically join in.

D. Eine gute Ausrede

As a follow-up activity, ask students to describe a situation in which they needed an excuse. What excuse did they give? Was it believed? What, if anything, did they get away with?

SPRECHAKTE: *DIE ABSICHT HABEN*

In preparation for the **Variationen**, read the dialogue for listening comprehension. Sample questions:

> **Wo möchte Carl-Heinz studieren?**
> **Was möchte er studieren?**
> **Was überrascht Otto?**
> **Was möchte Gabriele?**
> **Was ist ihr Problem?**

Before reading the dialogue a second time, ask:

> **Wie drückt man eine Absicht aus?**
> **Hören Sie sich die beiden Dialoge noch einmal an und schreiben Sie auf, wie die Sprecher Ihre Absicht ausdrücken.**

Collect expressions from students and list on the board. Then have students answer the following question quietly to themselves. Say:

> **Was haben Sie vor, wenn Sie mit Ihrem Studium fertig sind? Machen Sie sich Notizen.**

Then do a pair activity. Sample instructions:

> **Erklären Sie Ihrem Partner/Ihrer Partnerin, was Sie nach Beendigung Ihres Studiums vorhaben. Verwenden Sie die Ausdrücke an der Tafel. Machen Sie sich Notizen.**

Have a couple of students report to the class about their plans.

LESETEXT: EIN DEUTSCHER IN DEN USA

Cultural Note

Writers from German-speaking countries have frequently explored the United States as visitors, travelers, and exiles. Among the many writers who took refuge in this country during the Hitler regime were Bertolt Brecht, Franz Werfel, Heinrich and Thomas Mann, Lion Feuchtwanger, and Carl Zuckmayer. Only the last three became relatively "Americanized" and fared well during their years in exile. Thomas Mann, who held various well-paying positions in the States, became an American in 1944. Mann wrote perhaps the most important German work in American exile, the novel *Doktor Faustus* (1947). Zuckmayer's 1946 drama, *Des Teufels General,* was an instant success in postwar Germany and remained one of the most frequently performed plays for more than a decade. Contrary to Mann, Feuchtwanger, and Zuckmayer, most other writers, among them Bertolt Brecht, eked out a rather meager existence and felt alienated in their temporary surroundings.

After World War II, many German-speaking writers spent extended periods of time in the United States. Among the first accounts of such visitors is *Stiller*, a 1954 novel by the Swiss author Max Frisch, which is based on personal experiences gathered during a 1951–1952 trip to the United States and Mexico, where his 1957 novel *Homo faber* takes place. Frisch's 1974 chance encounter with an American woman 30 years his junior became the subject of his 1975 semi-autobiographic story, "Montauk."

The (West) German writer Martin Walser spent the summer of 1958 in the United States and has returned many times. Reflections of his relationship to this country can be seen in two of his novels, *Halbzeit* (1960) and *Brandung* (1985). The most important work of Uwe Johnson (1934–1984), the tetralogy *Jahrestage: Aus dem Leben von Gesine Cresspahl* (1970–1983), draws to a great extent on Johnson's year in New York (1967), which helped him establish the novel's two narrative planes, the German and the American.

The most important literary group of the postwar period, Gruppe 47 (founded by Hans Werner Richter in 1947), held its 1966 annual meeting at Princeton University, at which time Peter Handke, a young Austrian writer, delivered his now infamous piece of scathing criticism of this once trend-setting group. Handke used his experiences in the United States in his 1972 novel, *Der kurze Brief zum langen Abschied,* which, on the surface, was the description of a crosscountry journey. More recently, he incorporated material from the United States in his story, "Langsame Heimkehr" (1979). Another Austrian poet and writer, Ingeborg Bachmann (1926–1973), painted a positive, lyric picture of the city of New York in her famous 1958 radio play, *Der gute Gott von Manhattan.*

Writers of the former GDR were equally fascinated by the theme of America in their works, which often display a love–hate relationship colored more or less by official doctrine. An early exception is Stefan Heym's 1953 novel, *Goldsborough,* which draws heavily on Heym's years in the United States and his service in the U.S. Army. After Heym resettled in the GDR, this work was published there in 1954 in a German translation as *Goldsborough oder Die Liebe der Miss Kennedy*. At the end of the 60s, many GDR authors condemned the U.S. involvement in Vietnam. Anna Seghers (1900–1983), one of the most important writers of the GDR, who spent the war years in exile in Mexico and in 1947 resettled in East Berlin, commented on the aftermath of the Vietnam problem in her 1977 story, "Steinzeit."

Vor dem Lesen

A. Aktivieren Sie Ihr Hintergrundwissen

Use small groups. Have half the groups briefly discuss the first two questions and the other half the other two questions. Afterward, have all groups report back to the class.

B. Richtig oder falsch?

Have students in small groups discuss the nine questions and the first part of the text. They should then read the remainder of the text and do the other true/false questions, correcting those that are false, as homework. Repeat the process for the other parts of the text.

As an alternative, have students briefly summarize the content of part 1 or 2. Let them "feed" you key words from their summaries as you write them on the board. They may prepare their summaries as homework or in groups, but they should give them *orally* in class.

Nach dem Lesen

A. Kognate und „falsche Freunde"

Have the students do this activity in small groups, then discuss the meaning of the "false friends" briefly in plenum.

B. Schreiben Sie!

This may be done as homework or as a small-group activity in class. Additional questions on this text:

TEIL 1:
Wo kam Peter Schneider in den USA an?
Was für ein Auto hat er sich gekauft?
Was haben die Amerikaner über Peters Auto gesagt?
Warum war Peter in den USA?
Wie lange wollte Peter in den USA bleiben?
Was mußte er deshalb machen?
Woraus besteht die theoretische Prüfung?
Was hatte Peter nicht dabei?
Warum wollte der Autoverkäufer seinen Wagen noch vor Ende 1985 verkaufen?
Wo und wie fand die Prüfung statt?
Was wollte Peter, daß der Autoverkäufer macht?
Welche Grundregel erlernt man in den USA schon als Kind?
Was ist in Deutschland ein Massensport?
Wie kann es sich Peter nur erklären, daß in den USA das Schummeln so verpönt ist?
Welches Bild haben die Deutschen von Amerika?
Von wem wird die amerikanische Gesellschaft Peters Meinung nach regiert?
Warum hätte Nixon Peters Meinung nach gestürzt werden sollen?
Warum wurde er gestürzt?
Was brachte das amerikanische Volk gegen Reagan auf (1986)?
Was können die Europäer nicht richtig einschätzen?

TEIL 2:
Wie lange war Peter in Kalifornien?
Wo hat er einmal eine Nacht verbracht? Warum?
Wo wird „Trunkenheit am Steuer" härter bestraft, in Deutschland oder in den USA?
Mit wie vielen Leuten war Peter in einer Zelle? Was waren das für Leute?
Wie lange mußten die meisten Leute in dieser Zelle bleiben?
Was war der einzige Komfort?
Gab es in dieser Zelle soziale Spannungen? Wie erklärt sich das Peter?
Wogegen protestierte Peter sofort?
Wie fühlte er sich behandelt?
Was erklärten ihm seine Zellengenossen?
Wie würden das Linke in Deutschland interpretieren?
Wie interpretiert es Peter?

Kapitel 8

TEIL 3:
Was hält Peter von dem ständigen Hissen der amerikanischen Flagge?
Was ist für Peter das andere (d.h., das deutsche) Extrem?
Findet er das richtig?
Was mußte Peter viel machen? Wofür zum Beispiel?
Wie interpretiert er das?

Aktivitäten

B. Einkaufen macht Spaß!

Elicit from students the sequence of events and expressions in a buy/sell situation. Sample questions:

Was sagt der Kunde zuerst?
Was sagt der Verkäufer?
Was sagt der Kunde dann?

Provide information from your own experience, perhaps tell an anecdote. Review the model with students. Then have them work in pairs. Afterward, have a couple of pairs perform their dialogues. Discourage students from writing out the dialogue; encourage realistic speaking situations.

SPRECHAKTE: *GLAUBEN/ZWEIFEL*

Present the dialogues as listening comprehension exercises. Sample questions:

Dialogue 1: **Wer gibt eine Party? Warum kann Rainer nicht hin?**
Dialogue 2: **Wohin soll der Sohn gehen? Was hält der Vater davon? Warum?**

Drawing

Have students look closely at the drawing (p. 240). Ask them what is wrong with the girl's dress. From whose perspective is it a problem? Have they ever had similar problems with their parents?

Kapitel 9: Blick auf Deutschland

Opening Photo

Have students describe the photo (p. 254). Where is this? What do they see in the photo? What was the function of the wall?

EINSTIMMUNG: DEUTSCHLAND UND DIE DEUTSCHEN

As a preparation for the reading, draw an assoziogram for **Deutschland** and **deutsch**. Discuss the terms suggested by the students. Which are clichés? Which are facts? Which are suppositions/conclusions? Which are based on the experiences of students? Suggest alternatives or extensions when needed to provide a balanced picture.

LESETEXT: TYPISCH DEUTSCH?

Vor dem Lesen

Ask students about the different persons quoted in **Worte der Woche** and their approximate birth dates and ages.

Nach dem Lesen

A. Wer hat das gesagt?

This activity can be done as group work, then discussed in plenum.

Aktivitäten

C. Interaktion

It is important that students use as many different verbs as possible. They can narrate and report in the past at this level, but they will need practice. Have students work in small groups in which one student narrates or reports and the others listen for past tense verbs and forms. Then have one student come before the class and narrate while the other students write down all the verbs used. Afterward, write the infinitives and the participles of those verbs (and others) on the board.

LESETEXT: ZU GAST IN DER BUNDESREPUBLIK

Cultural Note

„Warum nicht deutsch?" addresses the problem of **Gastarbeiterdeutsch**, a linguistic phenomenon that has attracted much attention during the past 20 years. It is not uncommon to hear Germans simplify their speech by resorting to "infinitive sentences" such as **Du jetzt gehen ins Büro**, a tendency documented in this story. Germans often accommodate nonnative speakers either by speaking more slowly and distinctly or by speaking the foreigner's native language.

Vor dem Lesen

Introduce part 1 of the reading with a hypothetical scenario such as:

> Sie sind gerade in Deutschland angekommen, um ein Jahr lang dort zu studieren. Was brauchen Sie alles? Wohin müssen Sie dafür gehen? Was müssen Sie tun, um das zu bekommen (z.B. Wohnung, Geld, Bankkonto, Führerschein, Auto, Arbeitserlaubnis, Arbeit, Telefon)?

Introduce part 2 of the reading with a general discussion. Sample questions:

> Jede Sprache hat eine Variante, die für Ausländer gedacht ist: Wie sprechen Amerikaner, wenn sie z.B. mit Mexikanern sprechen, die nur wenig Englisch können?

Explain how Germans speak, particularly with **Gastarbeiter: du + Infinitiv + Ergänzung**. Ask:

> Was impliziert das „du": Respekt oder Respektlosigkeit/Herabwürdigung? Das „du" kann als Beleidigung verwendet werden oder als beleidigend empfunden werden.

Compare the use of "boy" with blacks during the first half of this century in the US.

Nach dem Lesen

A. Was steht im Text?

Have students read the first paragraph and then decide which of the three statements best reflects the content of the paragraph. Do a couple of these in plenum, then let students complete the work in groups. Repeat for each section of the text. As an alternative, have students complete the reading and this activity as homework.

B. Im Kreuzfeuer

This activity may be used as a poll or a questionnaire. Following the activity, write the affirmative answers on the board.

C. Fragen zum Text

This activity may be done individually in class as a writing exercise or as homework. The following additional questions are offered for further discussion of the text.

TEIL 1:

Was für Probleme haben Ausländer, die nach Deutschland kommen?
Wo, glaubt der Autor, kann man Deutsch lernen?
Wohin geht er mit dem chinesischen Professor?
Was braucht er? Wofür?
Mit wem spricht der Beamte meistens?
Was sagt er, wenn er schließlich doch mit dem Professor spricht?
Wie gut ist das Deutsch des Professors?
Versteht er den Beamten? Warum (nicht)?
Warum antwortet der Professor mit „ja"?
Was sagt daraufhin der Beamte? Wie heißt das in richtigem Deutsch?
Wie wird China noch genannt?
Wo bleiben der Autor und der Professor auf ihrem Stadtbummel stehen?
Warum gibt es keine Tafel neben der Tür?
In welcher Sprache antwortet der Mann, den der Autor um Informationen bittet? Warum?

TEIL 2:

Was möchte der Amerikaner?
Wohin fahren der Autor und der Amerikaner?
Mit wem sprechen sie?
Woher kommt der Amerikaner?
In welcher Sprache spricht der Amerikaner? in welcher sprechen die Deutschen?
Wie gut ist das Englisch der Deutschen?
Warum versteht der Vorsitzende den Amerikaner so gut?
Was für einen Rat gibt der Autor dem Amerikaner?
Wohin gehen die beiden am Abend? Was passiert da?

TEIL 3:

Wo ist der Autor? Wen trifft er da?
Wie gut ist das Deutsch dieser Person? Woher wissen wir das?
Was möchte diese Person tun? Warum? Was ist in Deutschland verboten?
Wie spricht die Dozentin mit dem Inder? Wie empfindet das der Inder?
Erklären Sie genau. Was hält der Inder von dem reduzierten Deutsch, dem Gastarbeiteridiom?
Was sagt die Kassiererin in der Cafeteria zu dem Inder?
Welchen Schluß gibt das dieser Geschichte?

Cultural Note

Rainer Maria Rilke (1875–1926), the most important and influential German lyric poet of the first half of the 20th century, spent 1905–1906 in Paris, primarily as private secretary of August Rodin, the famous French sculptor. Rilke mastered the French language, wrote poetry in it, and knew and corresponded with André Gide (1869–1951), some of whose works he translated.

LESETEXT: LYRIK

Cultural Note

„Die Deutschen" is a prime example of a Turkish writer's view of his German "hosts," which, in a few poignant stanzas, highlights the different perception of life and life's necessities that separates the Turkish from the German cultural sphere.

TEXT

To introduce the poem, read it aloud slowly. Have it printed on a transparency and reveal it line by line as you read. At several points stop and ask how the poem might continue. Encourage students to use their imagination and the gift of anticipation. Stop first after reading the first line. Ask, for example: Is the line positive or negative? Why is there an exclamation mark? Then read the poem a stanza at a time, asking questions about the content. After all stanzas have been read, cover the entire poem again and ask students to recall the content of each stanza. In this way you will be able to treat vocabulary as well as comprehension.

Nach dem Lesen

A. *Fragen zum Gedicht*

Do as group work, then discuss in plenum.

B. *Sichtwechsel*

Have students in small groups name key words and phrases needed for the poems. They should then write their poems as homework. Have several students read their poems, a few in each class period, over several days. An alternative topic might be „**Die USA aus deutscher Sicht."**

Aktivitäten

C. *Pantomimen!*

Have students form groups of five or six students. Taking turns, each student mimes a word from the list and asks: **Was habe ich gemacht?** The other students take turns guessing, using the present perfect in their answers. Continue until all words have been guessed. Use each word only once.

SPRECHAKTE: *LOBEN/MISSBILLIGEN*

Variationen

A. *Assoziogramme*

Make a list on the board. Sample questions:

> **Was sagt man, wenn man etwas gut findet? wenn man etwas schlecht findet?**

Use the dialogue as a listening comprehension exercise. Sample questions:

> **Wofür werden die Kinder gelobt? Wie werden sie gelobt?**

Add words or expressions to the list on the board.

Spielen Sie!

In preparation for this activity, each student should choose an article of clothing that he/she is wearing or a personal possession and ask other students what they think of it. Example:

> **Wie gefällt/gefallen dir meine Jacke/mein Rock/meine Schuhe?**

The student then writes down whether the answer is positive or negative. Whoever gets the most positive answers, wins. As an alternative, do as a recombination activity. Each student thinks of something that he/she has done recently and asks six students what they think of it. Insist that students use the present perfect tense in their responses. Model:

> **In meiner letzten Deutscharbeit habe ich ein A bekommen. Was sagst du dazu?**

The student then writes down whether the answer is positive or negative. Whoever gets the most positive answers, wins.

Thema IV: Macht euch die Erde untertan

Opening Photo

Ask students to describe what they see in the photo (p. 285). What contrasts are depicted? What emotions does the photograph evoke?

Kapitel 10: Des Deutschen liebstes Kind

Opening Photo

Using the photo (p. 286), do an associogram for **Verkehr.**

LESETEXT: CHAOS AUF DEN STRASSEN

Vor dem Lesen

As an introduction to the theme, have students tell anecdotes about their first time behind the wheel of a car. Alternatives for this activity:

A. A student with relatively good German relates an anecdote to the class and the class writes down the infinitives of all verbs used. Afterward, students name the participles of the verbs and list them on the board.
B. A student with relatively good German relates an anecdote to the class, and the class writes down all the conjunctions and adverbs used to join sentences or clauses.
C. Have students, in groups of three, relate anecdotes to one another. This will increase the amount of time students have to speak.

For a different introductory activity, students work in groups of four and compile lists of modes of transportation. For each mode of transportation have them come up with two advantages and two disadvantages. The group that comes up with the most modes of transportation within a given time limit (for example, 10 minutes) wins. Afterward, make a composite list of transportation types, listing advantages and disadvantages on the board.

Bring a map and have students find the major cities mentioned in the reading. Note that **Markt** is added to Bavarian place names to indicate that a town is larger than a village but smaller than a city.

Do an associogram for **Auto** on the board, and conduct a general discussion. Sample questions:

> Was wissen Sie über das Autofahren in Deutschland?
> Wie schnell darf man z.B. auf Autobahnen, auf Landstraßen, in der Stadt fahren?
> Was ist das in Meilen pro Stunde?
> Wie fahren die Deutschen?
> Warum, glauben Sie, fahren sie so?

Realia

Ask students to describe what they see in the realia entitled „**Die Unfall-Kurve**" (p. 288). Sample questions:

> Wann gab es mehr Unfälle, 1982 oder 1985?
> Wie viele Unfälle gab es 1986?

Cultural Note

West Germany, both before and after the 1990 unification, remains the only European country without any speed limits on the principal throughways, or **Autobahnen**. Although environmentalists and some politicians have been demanding a 130 km/h (approx. 80 mph) speed limit for years, most stretches of the **Autobahn** have only a **Richtgeschwindigkeit** (*recommended speed limit*). Older stretches in high-density areas have radar-controlled limits of 120 or 100 km/h. The speed limit on the **Bundesstraßen** (*federal highways*) is a poorly observed 100 km/h.

One of the most reliable sources of income for the former GDR was the heavily policed 100 km/h (approx. 60 mph) speed limit on all **Autobahnen**, including the transit sections to Berlin and Poland, which had been updated in the 1980s with financial help from the West German government. Speed traps were the rule. In addition, a time stamp on the transit visa of any motorist on a transit route could be checked against the time of arrival at the exit point, which would automatically indicate whether the motorist was traveling too fast or whether he/she stopped along the way to and from West Berlin. Nonetheless, on all but the upgraded sections, these speed limits have proven to be necessary: the 80 km/h limit on regular highways is simply a matter of survival in view of the severe disrepair of most of these roads.

The virtual "bloodbath" on the highways in the former East German territory is widely attributed to the loss of strict traffic controls and an influx of newer and faster West German cars. In spite of the fact that speed limits have been retained in the East German states, traffic fatalities increased by 74% in 1990. The sudden high volume of traffic, generally poor road conditions, speeding, and reckless driving are cited as prime factors. The German government has projected an outlay of about 127 billion marks for upgrading the rail and highway systems in the east, a job that will take at least a decade. In the meantime, no new construction can be undertaken.

Nach dem Lesen

A. *Überschriften suchen*

Have students call out possible titles and write their suggestions on the board. Correct the grammar as you go. Use the titles given to do a brief summary of the story.

B. *Neue Wörter im Kontext*

Have students suggest the meanings of the words, discussing structure when appropriate. Sample questions:

> Was ist der Infinitiv von *rasen*?
> Was für ein Verb ist es: regelmäßig oder unregelmäßig?
> Wie lautet also das Partizip Perfekt?
> Welches Hilfsverb wird verwendet: *haben* oder *sein*.

Realia

„Dem Wald zuliebe—freiwillig!" (p. 290). Sample questions:

> Wie sieht der Baum aus?
> Was soll die 100 bedeuten?

C. *Was meinen Sie?*

In groups of three or four, students should answer the questions, writing down key words. Discuss question No. 8 in plenum. Additional activity: **Was bedeuten die folgenden Kognate?**

> DER PSYCHOLOGE
> a. ein Mann, der sich mit menschlichem Verhalten beschäftigt
> b ein Mann, der sich mit Pflanzen und Bäumen beschäftigt
> c. ein Mann, der unter falschem Namen Artikel und Bücher schreibt

DAS CHAOS
a. besonderes Krankenhaus
b. Einkaufszentrum
c. völliges Durcheinander

DAS TEMPO
a. Geschwindigkeit
b. Fahrrad für zwei
c. südamerikanischer Tanz

DER LUXUS
a. ägyptische Stadt
b. etwas, was nicht nötig ist
c. wildes Tier, das im Wald lebt

DAS LIMIT
a. festgelegte Grenze
b. römischer Wall
c. seltener Edelstein

NEUROTISCH
a. erst kurz verheiratet
b. nicht normal, verrückt
c. neues Wort in einer Sprache

SUMMIEREN
a. zusammenzählen
b ein Geräusch verursachen
c. vergessen

KONTROLLIERT
a. gegen etwas, rückwärts
b. nicht erlaubt
c. das Gegenteil von frei

Aktivitäten

C. Partnerarbeit

Have students prepare this activity as homework. As a listening comprehension activity, describe your own thoughts about buying a new car. Have students write down useful vocabulary and expressions taken from your narration. As an alternative, have students form groups of six and take turns describing the car they want to buy. Each student takes notes and then decides with whom he/she would jointly purchase a car.

Cultural Note

While environmental pollution in many of the major metropolitan and industrial areas of western Germany is serious, it is significantly more so in the east. In contrast to West Germany, which has been environmentally conscious for several decades, East Germany virtually ignored environmental concerns, since cleaning the environment would have inevitably led to the closing of entire industries. In the process of political unification in 1990, the West and East German environmental ministers drew up a list of more than 400 plants that would need to be shut down and replaced. In this plan, for example, Bitterfeld near Halle will lose its notorious soft coal and chemical industry virtually overnight. The nuclear industry will fare no better: the Greifswald power plant in Mecklenburg, with its "Chernobyl-like" technology, has been decommissioned.

Lesetext: Wer fährt besser?

Cultural Note

In Germany, automobile insurance rates are not determined on the basis of gender. Even though women drivers cause statistically fewer and less expensive accidents, they do not receive special discounts on their auto insurance premiums.

Vor dem Lesen

Was meinen Sie?

Write **Männer** and **Frauen** at the top of the board in opposing corners. Have students give associations about male and female drivers. You may wish to begin by writing **schnell, langsam,** or **vorsichtig** in one column to see what reactions you get. Introduce the reading by saying:

> Im Text wird die Frage, wer fährt besser, beantwortet. Lesen Sie nur so weit, bis Sie die Antwort auf diese Frage wissen. Sobald Sie sie wissen, drehen Sie Ihr Buch um.

Nach dem Lesen

A. Richtig oder falsch?

Use small groups first, then discuss in plenum.

B. Vorurteile

As a follow-up to the reading and as a preparation for this activity, lead a short discussion:

> Welche Ihrer Argumente, die noch an der Tafel sind, werden im Text erwähnt?
> Welche zusätzlichen Argumente bringt er?
> Woher, glauben Sie, kommt das Vorurteil, daß Männer bessere Autofahrer sind?
> Denken Sie zum Beispiel daran, wenn Sie mit Ihrem Freund/Ihrer Freundin fahren: Wer fährt dann?
> Oder wenn Ihre Eltern zusammen im Auto fahren, wer fährt dann meistens?

SPRECHAKTE: VERLANGEN/BITTEN

Use the dialogue as a listening comprehension activity. Sample questions:

> Was wollen die Personen?
> Was genau sagen sie?

Kapitel 11: Umwelt—na und?

EINSTIMMUNG: AKTUELLE PROBLEME

Do an associogram for **aktuelle Probleme**. If time permits, continue with a brainstorming session in which students suggest possible solutions.

LESETEXT: VERKEHRTE WELT

Cultural Note

Because Germany is almost totally dependent on imported oil, it relies heavily on domestic coal production. While most of the coal mined in western Germany is high-quality anthracite (**Steinkohle**), most of the coal in the east is soft, or bituminous, coal (**Braunkohle**). In the east, strip mines are not uncommon. Owing to the cleaner-burning anthracite and stringently observed emission-control rules now long in place in the west, the coal-fired power plants there are more environmentally tolerable than those in the east, which remain a tremendous source of air pollution.

Early on, West Germany banked on atomic power plants for the generation of electricity. Currently, 35% of all electric power is produced by more than 20 **Kernkraftwerke.** Although (West) German atomic power plants employ much safer technology than that of the Chernobyl-type reactor used in the (East) German Greifswald plant, construction of such plants became a political issue long before the 1986 disaster, with the CDU favoring and the SPD (and the Greens) opposing the building and licensing of new installations. Still, atomic power plants continue to be built in Germany. After the Chernobyl disaster, even more stringent safety regulations were drawn up, which place the (West) German plants among the safest in the world. Nonetheless, many advocates of atomic power now consider this form of energy a stop-gap measure until new or alternative forms of energy are found.

Vor dem Lesen

To establish a context, lead a short discussion about the disaster at Chernobyl. Sample questions:

> **Erinnern Sie sich noch an Tschernobyl?**
> **Was ist dort passiert?**
> **Welche Auswirkungen hatte das auf Mitteleuropa? auf andere Teile der Welt?**

Nach dem Lesen

C. Diskussion

Do questions No. 1–4 orally in plenum, and summarize No. 5–6. Do a group activity in which students prepare for a debate (**Vorbereitung auf eine Debatte**). Divide the class into an even number of groups, ideally with three persons per group. Each group decides whether it is for or against atomic power and then states arguments against and support for atomic power. In case no group decides to be "pro," simply appoint two groups to represent this view. Then do a mock debate. Have the pro and con groups sit facing each other. Insist that all participate and contribute something to the debate.

Realia

Ask your students about the film advertisement (p. 318). Sample questions:

> **Was ist das?**
> **Wie heißt der Film?**
> **Was sieht man auf dem Plakat?**
> **Was für eine Art Film wird das sein?**

Aktivitäten

A. Ergänzen Sie das Raster!

Have students work alone, either in class or at home, to complete the chart. Discuss their answers and have them describe the drawings of trees and plants in class. Encourage students to include (relative) size, color, and even usefulness (**Wozu braucht man Blumen?**) in their descriptions.

C. Gefühle

As an alternative, have students write 15 to 20 adjectives that express feelings. Then have them categorize the adjectives appropriately. Students determine categories from their experience and on the basis of the nature of the adjectives chosen. This activity may be done as homework, alone silently in class, or in small groups.

D. Schreiben Sie!

Have students prepare the activity as homework. After they have answered all the questions, have them choose their four most interesting situations. In the next class session, have students ask four other students about the four chosen situations, take notes, and report in plenum.

E. Und was möchten Sie, bitte?

Set up the activity by eliciting expressions from students to produce a model for the interaction. Sample questions:

> **Gibt es etwas, was du immer bei dir hast? Was ist das?**

LESETEXT: UMWELTPROBLEME

Cultural Note

Switzerland, since 1848 a neutral country, managed to maintain its neutrality during the two world wars. This neutrality, combined with its fairly inaccessible terrain, has contributed to an element of conservatism among many Swiss citizens. In his story, Hohler targets conservative Swiss burghers. As in any satire, there is a kernel of truth in his allegations: Indeed, acid rain does not stop at international borders, and some of the pollution harming Swiss forests may well be imported from nearby countries like Czechoslovakia and, perhaps to a somewhat lesser degree, Germany.

Vor dem Lesen

A. Warum sterben die Bäume?

This activity works well as a pair activity.

B. Erschließen Sie den Text

Do this activity in small groups. After groups have worked through the activity, write the names on the board.

Nach dem Lesen

A. Wer sagt was?

Do as a pair activity, as individual silent work, or as homework. Follow with a short wrap-up discussion.

B. Diskussion

Do as a group activity.

SPRECHAKTE: AUFFORDERN/SICH WEIGERN

Read the dialogues to the class as a listening comprehension activity. Sample questions:

> Dialogue 1: Was möchte Walter? Warum? Erfüllt Max die Bitte? Warum (nicht)? Wie bittet Walter? Was sagt er? Wie schlägt ihm Max die Bitte ab?
> Dialogue 2: Was möchte Ingrid? Warum? Bekommt sie es? Warum (nicht)?
> Dialogue 3: Was ist Emmys Problem? Was möchte sie? Bekommt sie das? Warum (nicht)?

Then have students role-play the three situations without books. For example, say:

> **Jack, bitten Sie Karen, Ihnen ihr Auto zu leihen. Karen, lehnen Sie ab.**

Correct the most glaring errors, especially those that inhibit communication, and provide correct models.

Variationen

B. Spielen Sie!

Have students practice the situations in pairs and then role-play them without books in plenum.

Kapitel 12: Gestern war heute

EINSTIMMUNG: COMPUTERWELT

Do an associogram for **Computer**. Sample questions:

> **Was macht man mit Computern?**

Note:

> *word processing* = **Textverarbeitung**
> *data processing* = **Datenverarbeitung**
> *computer science as a field of study* = **Informatik**

Do a second associogram for the parts of a computer:

> **das Keyboard, der Monitor, die Festplatte** *[hard disk]*,
> **der Floppy, die Diskette, die (Grafik-)Karte, das Modem,**
> **der Drucker, das Kabel, die Maus**

Divide the class into two equal groups. The left side interviews the right side, using the questions in the text. Then, have them switch roles. Afterward, do a summary activity in which various answers are elicited from different students in plenum.

As an alternative, chart the answers statistically. Sample questions:

> **Wie viele haben einen Apple-Computer? einen IBM-Computer? einen IBM-kompatiblen Computer?**

Cultural Note

Advertising in print and on radio and television is subject to greater scrutiny and more regulations in Germany than in the United States. For instance, advertisers are not allowed to compare their products with the competition; comparative advertising does not exist. German textbook publishers have to avoid at all cost printing photographs in their books that display company signs, since the competition might construe this as **Schleichwerbung** ("*sneaky,*" or *implicit advertising*).

LESETEXT: COMPUTERWERBUNG

Vor dem Lesen

A. Merkmale von Werbetexten

Discuss the features with your students and deal with any vocabulary problems at this time.

B. Fachsprache der Computerwelt

Discuss or review computer vocabulary with your students. For example, ask:

> **Welche Teile hat ein Computer?**

Possible answers:

> **das Keyboard, der Monitor, die Festplatte, der Floppy, die Diskette, die (Graphik-)Karte, das Modem, der Drucker, das Kabel, die Maus**

Write the words on the board as the class suggests them. Then have small groups look for English words in the ad.

Cultural Note

Like many other technologies, personal computing was developed in the United States. Accompanying this new technology was new terminology. While German has taken over many of the new English words as loans, some new German words have been coined as well: **Schnittstelle** (*port*), **Laufwerk** (*disk drive*), **Festplatte** (*hard disk*), and **Text-/Datenverarbeitungssystem** (*word/data processing system*), to name a few.

A similar linguistic phenomenon took place in the GDR, although on a somewhat smaller scale. In the wake of the 1957 Sputnik launch and the triumph of Soviet space technology, a new East German space vocabulary was derived from Russian. For example, an East German astronaut was known as a "cosmonaut." Everyday vocabulary, as well, reflected institutions and phenomena particular to the GDR (see the listing on pp. 429–430). These words are easily identified as East German. Yet, many terms common to the entire German language area have different meanings in different areas, such as: **Demokratie, Sozialismus,** or **freie Wahlen,** among others.

Contrary to France, which passed a law requiring all imported goods to be labeled in French and to carry French instructions, Germany does not have such a law. Therefore, it is possible to purchase an item and receive only English instructions. Moreover, almost 20 years after the introduction of the first home computers, one can still buy computers without a German keyboard (that is, not only without the keys arranged according to the German norm but also without umlauted vowels and the ß).

Aktivitäten

A. Interaktion

As a game, form an even number of groups, ideally with three students per group. Each group chooses ten of the listed occupations and writes ten questions in the form:

> **Wie nennt man einen Mann/eine Frau, der/die einen Bus fährt?**

Then have two groups play against each other. Group A reads a question and group B has ten seconds to answer the question correctly. If group B answers correctly, it gets one point. The groups take turns asking questions. During the game, you should circulate among groups and make corrections as needed. Note particularly any problems with relative clauses and subordinate word order.

B. Kombinieren Sie!

Have students do this activity as homework. In a following class session in plenum, ask, for example:

> **Was kann man mit Schuhen machen?**
> Response: **binden**
> **Ja, man bindet die Schnürsenkel (Schnürbänder). Was noch?**
> Response: **wegwerfen**
> **Ja, richtig. Wenn die Schuhe kaputt sind, wirft man sie weg.**

As an alternative or follow-up, have students work in pairs, taking turns to form complete sentences of the type used above. The partner should pay close attention to the grammatical correctness of the utterance.

Kapitel 12

D. Assoziogramm

In preparation for this activity, ask questions like:

Was kann man alles mit einer Tür machen?

Do the associogram on the board. Have students work in groups of four. Each group does three to five verbs per noun. Put a composite list on the board to close the activity.

SPRECHAKTE: UMS WORT BITTEN/AUFZÄHLEN

Variationen

Spielen Sie!

For situation No. 3 (**Zimmervermittlung**), elicit questions from students and write them on the board in abbreviated form (complement + infinitive). Divide the class into two halves and let the students work first alone quietly. Group A writes down what type of room they are looking for, Group B writes down what kind of room they have to rent. Give students a few key words to make the information comparable:

Miete, Größe, Tiere erlaubt, nachts Besuch erlaubt, eigenes Bad/Toilette usw

As a recombination activity, let students in Group A look for a room among students in Group B. Stop the activity when three or four students have found rooms to rent.

LESETEXT: PROGRAMMIERER GESUCHT

Cultural Note

Eulenspiegel, a weekly satirical paper, was the most critical publication in the former GDR. Like so many living in totalitarian states, East German readers were well attuned to reading between the lines. "Das Ding im Hof" can be seen as a scathing piece of criticism of the ineptitude of a centralized bureaucracy in which the individual has lost all ambitions and at best is interested in small personal gains. *Eulenspiegel* often served as a court of last resort for many disgruntled East Germans who, in the paper's letters to the editor, openly voiced criticism of local or party mismanagement.

Vor dem Lesen

A. Vorhersagen machen

Make transparencies from the illustrations (pp. 350–351); use them to support this activity in class.

Realia

Ask your students questions about the chart (p. 349). Sample questions:

**In welchem Beruf arbeiten die Leute wohl mit Computern?
Wozu benutzen sie sie?**

Nach dem Lesen

B. Was ist passiert, und wann?

Do as a group activity, then do a wrap-up in plenum. As an alternative, prepare an outline of the text in sentences, writing each sentence on a 3 x 5 card. Give each student one card. Students must, while speaking only German, reconstruct the story by putting the sentences back into the correct sequence. Then students retell the story, each reading from his/her own card in the correct order. Have at least as many cards as you have students in the class. For added spice, include two or three sentences that are not part of the story, or give one student more than one card so that he/she must stand "in two places at once."

C. Hauptgedanke oder Detail?

Read the first paragraph of the text aloud and elicit answers from the class for this activity. Repeat with the other sections of the text.

Aktivitäten

A. Pläne machen

As an alternative or follow-up, have each student ask three other students questions and then decide which student he/she wishes to accompany to the movies. As an additional writing activity, have students describe a film they have seen recently. Sample instructions:

Beschreiben Sie einen Film, den Sie in letzter Zeit gesehen haben.

B. Telefongespräch

As an alternative, have students do writing exercises as homework, narrating the phone conversation in the imperfect and subjunctive. Do the first sentence with students, writing an appropriate beginning on the board:

Als das Telefon klingelte, hob Diana den Hörer ab und meldete sich mit ihrem Namen. Auf die Frage, ob Diana da sei, fragte sie, wer am Apparat sei. . . .

Or have students do the preceding writing exercise during class in groups of three. Circulate and provide corrections and constructive criticism.

SPRECHAKTE: THEMA WECHSELN/ZUSAMMENFASSEN

Variationen

A. Cartoon

Lead students in a discussion about the meaning-in-context of **übrigens** in the cartoon. In what other situations would **übrigens** fit? Discuss other words and phrases listed in the **Sprechakte.**

B. Spielen Sie!

As an alternative for No. 3 and to practice the present perfect tense, have students narrate what they did over their last vacation. In preparation for this activity, have students provide 15 to 20 verbs, which you write on the board and for which you elicit the participle and auxiliary verb. This may also be done as a pair exercise with a third student as observer, who makes a list of the verbs used (the student who uses the most verbs, wins). As a follow-up, let the observer tell all he/she can remember about the narration. The original narrator can then offer corrections.

Thema V: Kennzeichen D

Opening Photo

Compare the opening photo (p. 369) of the wall coming down with the Kapitel 13 lead photo (p. 370). Discuss the happenings of November 9, 1989. Ask your students where they were when they heard about the fall of the Berlin Wall. If it is available, show selections from the video "Ein Volk sprengt seine Mauern." You may wish to refer to Kapitel 6 as background for this chapter. Topics discussed: **Jugend in der ehemaligen DDR, FDJ und SED, Lebensstandard in der DDR.**

Kapitel 13: Berlin im geteilten Deutschland

Opening Photo

See suggestion for Thema V opening photo.

EINSTIMMUNG: WAS WISSEN SIE SCHON?

Was wissen Sie schon über die ehemalige DDR?

Help students activate knowledge they already have. This can be done with an associogram, mind-mapping techniques, or lists on the board. As a homework assignment for the following day, have students think about the questions before they return to class. As an additional activity, do an associogram for **Berlin.**

LESETEXT: EIN SPAZIERGANG IN OST-BERLIN

Cultural Note

„Treffpunkt Weltzeituhr" provides valuable background information on the one-sided regulations that had first enabled West Germans and, not until later, West Berliners, to visit their friends and relatives in East Berlin (**Besucherregelung**).

Some of the small chicaneries, such as, the **Zwangsumtausch** (*required money exchange;* Western term) or **Mindestumtausch** (*minimum exchange;* Eastern officialese) are mentioned. Anyone visiting East Germany was required to exchange DM 25,- at a rate of one west for one east mark, which made it especially difficult for the elderly to visit their relatives more frequently. Because of the limited range of goods that one could purchase for these 25 marks, western visitors frequently went to the exclusive hotels and spent the **Zwangsumtausch** on a decent meal, the price of which was beyond the reach of the average East Berliner. Books or classical records, at times from other East bloc countries, were also often a good investment provided one could find interesting titles. The prices for many basic commodities and lower quality meals were subsidized. For example, a cup of coffee cost 83 Pfennig. (No tip was required in East Germany, since waiters were state employees and, therefore, above the "decadent" custom of tipping. Of course, this reinforced a lack of incentive to give good and speedy service.) The one-day restriction of the visit required visitors to leave East Berlin by midnight, a curfew that at times was so strictly observed that even a late arrival by a few minutes at the checkpoint could entail serious consequences. These are just a few examples of the difficulties West Germans (and West Berliners) had to contend with when visiting East Berlin or East Germany. The article indicates a certain softening of the East German authorities vis-à-vis some of the Western, "decadent" attributes that more recently were tolerated to appease a segment of the younger population.

Over the years, the West Berlin Senate (the governing body) pursued a policy of small, incremental relaxation of the East German visiting and travel restrictions. Early in 1989 (and thus a few months before the Wall came down), the East German authorities began to permit West Berliners to take their dogs with them on one-day visits to the eastern part of the city, provided the visitors could show the internationally required vaccination papers. Given the great number of old people involved in such one-day visits who did not want to leave their pets alone for the day, the Senate considered this a "minor victory."

Vor dem Lesen

Ask if anyone is familiar with the **Weltzeituhr.** What does it look like? What can you see on it?

Nach dem Lesen

A. Was steht im Text?

As an alternative, have students read the sentences *before reading* the text. Then do a timed reading of 10 to 12 minutes. Encourage students to ignore any glosses at this point. They should return to the activity and mark the sentences as true or false. Have students work in pairs to compare their answers. If a student disagrees with his/her partner, they may return to the reading to find out which one is correct.

Cultural Note

Wartburg and **Trabant** (or **Trabbi**, as their East German owners endearingly called the car) were the only two cars to be produced in the GDR, according to the grand COMECON plan drawn up in the 1950s and 1960s for the purpose of assigning industrial production in the East bloc. This master plan centralized the production of major industrial goods like buses, which were almost exclusively built in Hungary ("Ikarusz" buses were used in East Berlin), streetcars, trucks, and automobiles (heavy trucks were built primarily in the Soviet Union; Czechoslovakia produced a car called the "Skoda").

The Wartburg, the more technically "advanced" East German car, had a four-cylinder engine. In contrast, the Trabant, with a top speed of 60 mph, sported a two-stroke, two-cylinder motor in a fiberglass body. Still, many East Germans waited up to 15 years to take delivery of a "Trabbi." The style of the car had not changed in more than 25 years, and there was relatively little risk in ordering one, provided one had the steep down payment required. The free access of great numbers of "Trabbis" to the West German high-speed Autobahnen, where they virtually block the right lane, forcing even trucks into the passing lane at the slightest of grades, has created unheard-of traffic jams. Pollution from the two-stroke engines is another serious problem: All "Trabbis" were officially exempted from any pollution control regulations, and the new German government is hoping that the number of Trabants on the road (about 2 million in East Germany in 1990) will dwindle over the next few years. Production of the "Trabant" (see photo on p. 438) was virtually halted in mid-1990.

Aktivitäten

A. Erzählen Sie!

Such "story boards" may be used several times with different emphases: once in the present tense, later in the simple past tense.

B. Erzählen Sie weiter!

Encourage students to move from simple sentences, one-word, or phrase answers to connected discourse. Practice this technique by using the story board in **Aktivität A** or the questions in this activity in several stages, perhaps over several days. Stage 1: Solicit possible descriptions or narratives for each frame or question from various students. Stage 2: Use a "chain" technique, having students retell the story together, using the illustrations as a guide. Stage 3: Have several students, one at a time, do an extended narration/connected discourse with the illustrations as a guide. Stage 4: Have several students, one at a time, do the narration without visual support.

C. Was meinen Sie?

Use a technique similar to that described for **Aktivität B** to have students narrate a story based on the illustrations. Encourage students to use imagination and humor. Suggested descriptions:

> **Bild 1:** The husband didn't like the sermon and says so.
> **Bild 2:** The airport security guard is checking the woman's suitcase. What does he find? Is she in trouble or just embarrassed?
> **Bild 3:** The man is repairing a clock and can't figure out how to get it back together. What will he do with the "leftovers"?
> **Bild 4:** The mechanic is explaining that the repairs will cost more than anticipated. How does the woman react? What does she decide?

D. Sprichwörter

Proverbs are an excellent point of departure for narration. As an alternative, have students select a second proverb (That is, one he/she did not use in class) and write a narration based on that proverb.

LESETEXT: ÜBER DIE MAUER

Cultural Note

Peter Schneider's parody of the many serious accounts of East Germans desperately trying to cross the Wall once again evokes the psychosis from which many people were suffering as a consequence of having been "walled in" and locked in for almost three decades. The story uses much of the technical "border" vocabulary that has enriched the German language since the 1960s.

The new German government is trying to reuse the huge installations built by the East Germans at the checkpoints around Berlin. At such crossing points, the former GDR issued and/or checked transit visas and receipts (see realia, p. 384), after what often seemed to be interminable waiting periods. One of the more serious proposals for the "rededication" of these installations is to rebuild them into "Park-and-Ride" facilities for the ever-increasing number of commuters into Berlin.

Vor dem Lesen

A. Grenzen and B. Ableitungen

To get at the meaning of these words, ask students **Was ist das?** Have them use paraphrases, circumlocutions, or relative clauses to explain what these words mean. Sample definitions:

> **Ein Grenzer ist ein Grenzposten, also jemand, der (an der Grenze aufpaßt.)**
> **Was macht ein Grenzprovokateur?**
> **Eine Staatsgrenze ist eine Grenze, die (zwei Staaten voneinander trennt.)**
> **Wo gibt es eine Staatsgrenze in den USA? und in der Bundesrepublik? (Unterschied zwischen Bundesstaaten in den USA und Bundesländern in der BRD.)**

Nach dem Lesen

A. Überschriften formulieren

Here are some possible titles:

> **Absatz 1: Kabe springt von West nach Ost über die Mauer.**
> **Absatz 2: Kabe wollte nur auf die andere Seite und hat keine politischen Motive.**
> **Absatz 3: Kabe kommt in der DDR in eine psychiatrische Klinik.**
> **Absatz 4: Drei Monate später kommt er nach West-Berlin zurück.**
> **Absatz 5: Die Presse reagiert unterschiedlich auf den Mauerspringer.**
> **Absatz 6: Kabe kommt von seiner Reise aus Paris zurück und springt gleich wieder.**
> **Absatz 7: Kabe kommt nicht ins Gefängnis, weil die Bundesregierung die Grenze offiziell für illegal hält.**
> **Absatz 7: Kabe kommt in eine Westberliner psychiatrische Klinik.**
> **Absatz 8: Nach der Entlassung aus dieser Klinik springt er noch fünfzehnmal.**
> **Absatz 9: Motive für seine Sprünge gibt es nicht.**

Aktivitäten

B. Märchen

Fairy tales are an excellent point of departure for narration, since most of them are well known to students. As an alternative, students can write a modern fairy tale. After reading the modern fairy tales, the teacher may select a few to be read, or better, told to the entire class. You may also wish to tell the class these modern fairy tales as listening comprehension exercises.

SPRECHAKTE: ERZÄHLEN/BERICHTEN

Variationen

Often the present tense, sometimes called the "historical present," is used to lend immediacy to the narration of a past event. Have students relate the same story twice, once in the present tense and once in the past. Which do they like better? Which is more interesting, exciting, or immediate?

Kapitel 14: Das tausendjährige Reich

Opening Photo

Ask students what they recognize in the picture. Provide German vocabulary necessary to talk about what they see: **Hakenkreuz, Fahne, Uniform, Schnurrbart,** and so on.

EINSTIMMUNG: GESCHICHTE

A. *Assoziationen*

Do an associogram for **Das Dritte Reich**. Use the realia to "jog" students' memories. What feelings do the posters evoke? What are possible goals of the posters? For which parties are the posters? What is the significance of **Liste 1, Liste 3,** and **Liste 4?**

The parties represented are:

  Liste 1: Nationalsozialisten
  Liste 1: Sozialdemokraten
  Liste 3: KPD = Kommunistische Partei Deutschlands
  Liste 4: Zentrum

B. *Was wissen Sie?*

Assign preparation of this activity for homework. Suggest to your students that they look in a general world history text or an encyclopaedia to find the answers. Let students first discuss their answers in small groups, then discuss their responses in plenum.

LESETEXT: ES SPRICHT DER FÜHRER

Cultural Note

This excerpt, from a much longer speech to a select group of some 400 representatives of the German National-Socialist press, unmasks Hitler for the first time. In front of his timidly applauding audience, he admits to having been forced to speak of peace for decades to prepare the German people for war. He now appeals to the NS press corps to "reprogram" these same people for war. As a matter of fact, the specter of total war is raised in the concluding passages of this speech, which have not been reproduced here. In a brutality and explicitness unheard of until then, this speech culminates in Hitler's prediction that either there would be total victory or that the German people would perish along with him. It is clear that this speech was not publicly disseminated; as a matter of fact, it was virtually unknown until well into the 1960s. The elite journalists invited, many of them completely overwhelmed by what Hitler evoked in front of their eyes, were forbidden to discuss what they heard, and it seemed that many were hoping that this worst-case scenario simply would not happen after all, since they had every reason to believe in the **Endsieg** (*final victory*) the dictator prophesied.

Vor dem Lesen

Hintergrundwissen

Sample questions on the Treaty of Versailles:

> Wozu gehört Elsaß-Lothringen heute?
> Welchem Land gehört heute der größte Teil der Halbinsel Jütland?
> Wer waren die Sieger des Ersten Weltkrieges?
> Wer war am Ersten Weltkrieg beteiligt?
> Wo hatte Deutschland Kolonien?
> Wie begann der Erste Weltkrieg?

Sample questions on National Socialism:

> Welche Regierungsform hatte Deutschland vor und im Ersten Weltkrieg, welche zwischen 1919 und 1933?
> Seit wann gab es keine Wehrpflicht in Deutschland?

TEXT

Have students read the speech „Hitler vor Vertretern der deutschen Presse am 10. November 1938" in small groups, looking specifically for geographical areas. Have them find the areas mentioned on the map (p. 402). You may "float" from group to group and provide needed vocabulary.

Aktivitäten

A. Assoziogramme

Assign one associogram to each of four groups. Then, in plenum, put the associograms on the board, allowing other groups to contribute additional items to each one.

B. Gruppenarbeit

Have groups focus on specific questions: What is the implication of the man being "hooded" for the "winter"? Who is in control here? Why? What is the significance of calling the plant **"Liebling"**?

D. Gruppenarbeit

In preparation for this activity, help students think of possible films. Suggestions: "Gone with the Wind," "Reds," "Dangerous Liasons," a western with cowboys and Indians, a World War II film, a Vietnam era film like "Platoon" or "Full Metal Jacket," a cops-and-robbers film like "Dick Tracy" or "The Untouchables," a gangster film like "The Godfather," a fantasy like "Star Wars" or "Star Trek: The Movie."

E. Propaganda

Do some brainstorming about what kinds of articles students might want to bring. Suggestions: a real estate brochure, junk mail offering credit cards or health insurance, ads for products like cigarettes or alcohol, political advertisements, and so on.

LESETEXT: ROMAN EINER KARRIERE

Cultural Note

Klaus Mann's novel may be known in this country through the film, "Mephisto," an excellent Hungarian-German coproduction of 1981, in which the Austrian actor Klaus Maria Brandauer ("Out of Africa") played Hendrik Höfgen. The film dealt rather objectively with the dichotomy in the life of Gustaf Gründgens (1899–1963), the fascinating actor, producer, and director whose problematic life inspired Klaus Mann's novel to a certain degree. "Mephisto" showed Höfgen/Gründgens saving actors and friends from Nazi persecution while at the same time kowtowing to Goebbels, Hitler, and other Nazi powers in order to continue his triumphant productions at the government-sponsored **Staatliche Schauspielhaus Berlin**. Gründgens, director of this most important Berlin theater from 1934–1945, also directed a now classic film version of "Faust" (1960), in which he himself played the role of Mephisto (photo, p. 408).

TEXT

As a preparation or wrap-up activity, show an excerpt from the film "Mephisto" with Klaus Maria Brandauer as Hendrik Höfgen or a cut from the filmed stage version of Goethe's "Faust" with Gustav Gründgens as Mephisto. These films are available for rent at many local video stores.

This text is extremely complex, almost like a poem. Have students read the text silently first, ignoring any glosses. Then read the text aloud, pausing at appropriate places to check comprehension.

Aktivitäten

B. Was passiert?

In preparation for this activity, review the cartoon strip with students before assigning it as homework. Clarify the frames for the students:

Frame 1: She is tasting the cookies.
Frame 2: He is tasting the cookies.
Frame 3: She leaves the room crying.
Frame 4: He tries to "make up."

Ask students about the feelings of these people, about what they might be saying. Discuss their relationship: married? friends? lovers? siblings?

Tell students to prepare possibilities as homework, then let them put together the dialogue in small groups in class. You may want to collect and correct the dialogs before having samples read in class in the following class session.

Kapitel 15: Deutsche Perspektiven

EINSTIMMUNG: UNTERSCHIEDE ZWISCHEN OST UND WEST

Realia

Use questions and answers to get to the statistics reflected here. Begin with cognates of the more obvious categories (**politisch interessiert, freundlich, aktiv, religiös**) before moving to more problematic ones (**bescheiden, aufgeschlossen, selbstbewußt**). Provide students with examples to explain the more obscure terms rather than giving English translations.

Cultural Note

The **Eigenschaftsprofile** (*attitudinal profiles*) reflect views of West and East Germans' attributes as seen by (West) German young adults ages 14 to 21. The West German opinion poll did—and could—not canvas the corresponding East German age group. For this reason, some of the results (for instance, East Germans are perceived to be completely "unbureaucratic" in comparison with West Germans) are somewhat impressionistic. Nonetheless, these profiles provide a good measure of what young West Germans thought of their own (older) compatriots in comparison with the (perceived) "average" East German two years before the Wall came down.

LESETEXT: BEIDERLEI DEUTSCHE—ZWEIERLEI DEUTSCHE

Vor dem Lesen

Damals und heute

Have students prepare this activity in pairs. Put the two headings **damals** and **heute** on the board. Have students come forward, one at at time, and write the words in the appropriate column.

Cultural Note

The **Neue Heimat** real estate holding organization in Hamburg was Europe's largest company specializing in the development of large housing projects and of entire suburbs. Founded in 1926, it was owned by the (West) German **Gewerkschaften** (*labor unions*) and union banks. After years of scandalous management, it was sold off in the late 1980s. Many of the **Neue Heimat** housing projects of the 1950s and 1960s resemble the monotonous, prefabricated GDR developments that only very recently began to sport different color facades. More recent **Neue Heimat** projects—and this is where the kindly comparison made by the Hamburg visitor no longer holds true—were much more sophisticated, differentiated, and sociologically more acceptable.

Cultural Note

The "**Deutsch-deutsches Diktionär,**" while mostly self-explanatory, lists a strange combination of official terms or acronyms (**AFG, Delikat-Läden, EOS, Kader,** and so on) along with popular, tongue-in-cheek neologisms for which Berliners in both East and West are so famous: **Bückware** is a take-off on **Backware** (*baked goods*), implying that the salesperson has to bend down under the counter (**bücken**) to unearth hidden, scarce items; **Rostlaube** (literally, *rusty gazebo*) indicates the standard of rustproofing of a "Moskwitsch," a Russian middle-size car (the term is not new, though); **Zootechniker** (*zoo technician*) for farm hand is the same kind of euphemism that can be seen in West German word creations like **Raumpflegerin** (*a woman taking care of interior space*) for the much less attractive, older designations **Reinemachefrau** and **Putzfrau** (*cleaning woman*).

Nach dem Lesen

As a follow-up activity, lead a discussion. Sample questions:

> Welche damals typischen Bilder in der DDR könnten sich ein paar Jahre nach Öffnung der Mauer und Einheit mit Westdeutschland schon geändert haben? Bei welchen dauert es länger?

Aktivitäten

A. Tatsachen

Answers to questions:

1. **Ostberlin**
2. **Berlin**
3. **SED = Sozialistische Einheitspartei Deutschlands**
4. **in der ehemaligen DDR**
5. **in der Schweiz**
6. **67 000 000 in (West) Deutschland; 17 000 000 in der (ehemaligen) DDR; insgesamt ungefähr 83 000 im vereinten Deutschland**
7. **1971**
8. **in der Schweiz**
9. **in (West) Deutschland**
10. **die Bundesrepublik Deutschland oder die Schweiz**

LESETEXT: EINE DDR-SCHRIFTSTELLERIN IM WESTEN

Cultural Note

Gabriele Eckart's interesting article presents an intriguing account of a critical GDR citizen's view of both former German states: The author does not appreciate many of the West German "accomplishments" and is justly critical of the superficiality of many of the West Germans she meets, but her return to her native GDR is marred by immediate—and disillusioning—confrontations with the many ineptitudes of that country's service systems. Gabriele Eckart now teaches at a major American university.

Vor dem Lesen

A. „Ein DDR-Indianer im Wilden Westen"

Do as an associogram on the board.

B. (Untitled)

Have students silently mark which things they associate with the Federal Republic or with the former German Democratic Republic. Then list them in two columns on the board and have students support their selections. For example:

Werbung: BRD, weil es in der DDR praktisch keine Produktwerbung gab.

Ask:

Wobei handelt es sich um Tatsachen, wobei um Klischees?

Nach dem Lesen

B. Information ordnen

Positives: viele Früchte und Blumen, ausländische Sänger, Schaufenster von Reisebüros und Buchläden, frei sprechen können, keine Zensur, Bäume nicht so krank, Freizügigkeit

Negatives: zuviel des Guten, jeder will ihr immerzu etwas verkaufen, Buch als Ware, zu viele Autos, Autolärm, Reklame, zu viel Zivilisation, keine Widerstände, Publikum übersättigt, wenig Interesse für die DDR, zu geräuschvoll, zu schnell.

APPENDIX

ACTFL Proficiency Guidelines

1. Functional Trisection of Proficiency Levels for Speaking

PROFI-CIENCY LEVEL	FUNCTION	CONTEXT	ACCURACY
Novice	no functional ability; communicates minimally with memorized isolated words and phrases	none	unintelligible
Intermediate	creates with the language by combining and recombining learned elements mostly in a reactive mode; asks and answers questions; can initiate, sustain, and close short basic conversations; can therefore function in basic social survival situations	courtesy requirements and basic information about self; survival topics; leisure activities	intelligible to sympathetic native speaker used to dealing with foreigners; frequent pauses and unexpected attempts at circumlocution that are not always successful
Advanced	converses in a clearly participatory fashion; completes a wide variety of communicative tasks even when they become involved due to complications and unforeseen turns: can complain, apologize, and elaborate; narrates and describes in detail with paragraph-length connected discourse; can therefore function successfully in everyday as well as routine work and school situations	topics of current public interest; topics related to particular personal interests and special fields of competence	clearly understandable to native speaker not used to dealing with foreigners; may miscommunicate; no firm grasp of interactive and discourse strategies; still needs to rely heavily on communicative strategies, but they usually work
Superior	functions in most types of formal and informal conversations; supports opinions and hypothesizes, using native-like discourse strategies	practical, social, professional, and all but the most abstract and unfamiliar specialized topics	the few mistakes that occur do not disturb the native speaker or interfere with communication; cannot always tailor language to audience

2. Functional Trisection of Proficiency Levels for Listening

PROFI-CIENCY LEVEL	FUNCTION	CONTEXT	ACCURACY
Novice	no functional ability; understands only short learned utterances in face-to-face situations	none	requires long pauses, repetition, rephrasing, and generally reduced rate of speech
Inter-mediate	understands sentence-length utterances that consist of recombinations of learned utterances in face-to-face conversations, routine telephone conversations, and simple announcements and reports over the media; comprehends instructions and directions	basic personal background and needs, survival situations, social conventions; some personal activities and interest areas	misunderstanding of main ideas and/or details common; understanding usually bound to the situation
Advanced	understands descriptions and narrations in different time frames and aspects; interviews; short lectures; news items; and reports dealing with factual information	familiar topics of everyday life and routine work situations	occasional inability to use cohesive devices to follow the thought sequence of an oral text; frequent inability to grasp sociocultural nuances of a message
Superior	understands main ideas of all discourse, including the essentials of proposition-ally and linguistically complex oral texts that occur—for example, in academic settings; shows some appreciation of aesthetic norms, idioms, colloquialisms, register shifting of the target language; can make inferences within the cultural framework of the target language; shows some sociocultural sensitivity	all speech in a standard dialect, including technical discussions in a field of specialization	misunderstandings occasionally occur when speech is excessively rapid, or highly colloquial, or has strong cultural references
Distin-guished	understands all—due to strong sociocultural and audience awareness	all contexts	some difficulty with some dialects and slang

ACTFL Proficiency Guidelines

3. Functional Trisection of Proficiency Levels for Reading

PROFI-CIENCY LEVEL	FUNCTION	CONTEXT	ACCURACY
Novice	recognizes cognates and borrowed words; starts to understand short written messages in highly standardized and contextualized situations, when vocabulary has been learned	areas of practical need, such as basic survival situations: some items on a menu, a map, a timetable	rereading frequently required
Inter-mediate	understands linguistically simple, connected texts that have a clear underlying internal structure, such as simple descriptions of persons, places, things	basic personal and social needs, as long as the social needs are of interest to the reader, or he or she has some knowledge of them	misunderstandings may occur, rereading may be necessary
Advanced	understands prose of several paragraphs in length if there is a clear underlying structure and if the prose is in familiar sentence patterns; understanding derives less from situational and subject-matter knowledge and more from control of the language; texts include short stories, news items, notices, correspondence	personal, social, routine work, everyday and simple literary situations	gets main ideas but may miss or misunderstand some details
Superior	reads with almost complete comprehension and at normal speed expository prose that features hypotheses, argumentation, and supported opinions, and includes structures and vocabulary usually encountered in academic or professional reading; texts include literary texts, reports, editorials, correspondence	unfamiliar subjects encountered in professional, academic, and literary texts as well as technical material	some difficulty with unusually complex structures and rare idioms; rereading is rarely necessary, and misunderstanding is rare
Distin-guished	comprehends most styles and forms, due to understanding of nuance, subtlety, author intent, and unpredictable turns of thought	all except for unfamiliar specialized material not directed to the general reader	usually complete comprehension

4. Functional Trisection of Proficiency Levels for Writing

PROFI-CIENCY LEVEL	FUNCTION	CONTEXT	ACCURACY
Novice	no communicative writing skills except starting to be able to supply names, dates, numbers, nationalities, and some other learned phrases on simple forms; can copy and reproduce some familiar words and phrases	none except maybe basic personal information to be furnished on forms necessary for immediate survival	spelling often only partially correct
Inter-mediate	can take simple messages and write simple short texts consisting of a loose collection of sentences without cohesive devices or signs of conscious organization	practical writing needs and some very limited social demands; personal information, daily routine, everyday events, topics grounded in personal experience	understandable to natives used to the writing of nonnatives; spelling and grammatical mistakes frequent
Advanced	joins sentences in simple discourse of several paragraphs in length; uses limited number of cohesive devices; organization is emerging; texts include note-taking, summaries, résumés	social correspondence; informal business correspondence; personal experience in detail; concrete aspects of topics of particular interest and of special fields of competence	understandable to natives not used to the writing of foreigners; expression with circumlocution; style still distinctly foreign; good control of basic morphology and grammatical structures; often strong in either vocabulary or grammar, but never in both
Superior	hypothesizes, presents arguments and points of view; underlying organization strongly evident; sensitive to differences in formal and informal style; texts include most types of correspondence, short research papers, and statements of position	most formal and informal writing on practical, social, and professional topics that fall into the writer's area of expertise	errors rarely disturb natives or cause miscommunication; good control of all grammatical structures; vast vocabulary; not always able to tailor a text to purpose and/or reader